HYPOCRITES

★ ★ ★ & ★ ★ ★

HALF-WITS

HYPOCRITES

&

HALF-
WITS

A DAILY DOSE OF SANITY
FROM CAFE HAYEK

DONALD J. BOUDREAUX

Hypocrites & Half-Wits: A Daily Dose of Sanity from Cafe Hayek
was produced by Free To Choose Press,
Erie, Pennsylvania.

Don Boudreaux, Author
James Tusty, Project Leader
Bill Crawford, Aaron Hierholzer, James Tusty, Editors
Neil Gonzalez, Designer
Phil Heidenreich, Image Research Assistant

Distributed by Emerald Book Company

For ordering information or special discounts for bulk purchases, please contact Emerald Book Company at PO Box 91869, Austin, TX 78709, 512.891.6100.

Publisher's Cataloging-In-Publication Data

(Prepared by The Donohue Group, Inc.)

Boudreaux, Donald J.

   Hypocrites & half-wits : a daily dose of sanity from Cafe Hayek / Donald J. Boudreaux. -- 1st ed.

   p. : ill. ; cm.

   A collection of 111 of Boudreaux's best letters to editors of major American publications. These letters were originally posted on the author's blog.

   ISBN: 978-0-9839687-0-2

   1. United States--Politics and government--21st century--Miscellanea. 2. United States--Economic conditions--Miscellanea. 3. Letters to the editor--United States--21st century. 4. Boudreaux, Donald J.--Correspondence. I. Title. II. Title: Hypocrites and half-wits III. Title: Cafe Hayek. Selections.

JK275 .B68 2012

320.973   2011944622

Published in the United States by Free To Choose Press, an educational initiative of Free To Choose Network. Free To Choose Network is a not-for-profit 501(c)3 U.S. corporation.

Free To Choose Press
2002 Filmore Avenue
Erie, PA 16506
www.freetochoose.net

OUR PURPOSE / To use accessible and entertaining media to build popular support for personal, economic and political freedom. We believe these freedoms are interdependent and must be sustained by the rule of law.

12 13 14 15 16 10 9 8 7 6 5 4 3 2 1

First Edition

Getting on Don's E-mail List

Don writes a letter a day to the editor, and he sends out each day's letter to his followers via e-mail. If you would like to receive Don's daily e-mails, sign up at www.donaldjboudreaux.com.

Comments

Don has a hotline for those who wish to tell him how much they agree with him, or how much he is an idiot. Call (530) 324-5278 and leave Don a message. He listens to all of them personally.

*To Thomas, a young scientist keenly on guard
against hypocrites and half-wits*

PREFACE

....

Many years ago my family ordered me to remove my shoes before sit-
ting down to watch the evening news on television. They feared that
I'd fling my loafers or sneakers through the TV screen. This fear was
justified because—I'm embarrassed to confess—I get unduly agitated by
rank economic ignorance parading publicly as expert knowledge. Sel-
dom had I spent 30 minutes of any given evening watching the likes of,
say, Dan Rather without my wanting to throw my shoe at his face after
he uttered some absurd economic fallacy as if it were established and
undisputed truth.

The electronic and print media—and now, of course, also cyber-
space—have long been, and continue to be, chock-full of nonsense
about economics. And I mean here not advanced economic theory, but,
rather, basic and foundational stuff. Pick up almost any newspaper or
magazine, or visit almost any news or opinion site on the Internet, and
you will find there a dense jungle of economic misunderstandings.

So rather than destroy my family's television, I began venting my
frustration by writing letters to editors—and letters to newscasters,
news-programming directors, and sometimes even to politicians.

This practice has proven to be more peaceful and, I think, productive than shoe-throwing. Over the past decade or so I've written close to 5,000 such letters. Most are very short—fewer than 200 words—and many have been published in the pages of the *Wall Street Journal*, the *New York Times*, the *Washington Post*, the *Atlantic*, the *Economist*, and other publications, from the august to the now-defunct.

Starting in 2004, some—though by no means all—of my letter have appeared at the blog I do with my friend and colleague Russell Roberts, Cafe Hayek (www.cafehayek.com).

But more important than my blog, e-mail has enabled me to accost many of my friends with my daily letters. I keep a long list of e-mail addresses to which I send each of my letters soon after I write it. (If you'd like to be added to my e-mail list, I'll be both pleased and honored to sign you up. Just go to www.donaldjboudreaux.com.) These friends often write back with constructive criticisms that have helped me over the years to improve not only my writing but also my own understanding of economics, history, politics, and current events. I thank them all here, deeply.

Several of those friends eventually started telling me "You should publish your letters in a book." This advice flattered me, of course, but I couldn't get my mind around just how such a book would work.

Enter Jim Tusty.

Jim—a successful businessman and filmmaker—got on my "letters list" through our mutual friend Bob Chitester, founder of the Free To Choose Network. It is Jim and Bob who finally persuaded me to compile some of my letters into the book that you now hold in your hands.

More importantly, it's Jim who did the lion's share of the detailed work necessary to make this book a reality. From narrowing the selection of letters from thousands to 100—to compiling many of the materials that appear on each letter's facing page—to arranging funding for this project, with much-appreciated help from Bob—to, well, nearly every phase of production of the book, Jim has been indispensable. I do not exaggerate.

Truth be known, Jim should be listed as a coauthor.

So my biggest thanks go to Jim. Were I to express those thanks as fully as I should, this Preface would run on way too long. Just know that I know that this book wouldn't exist without Jim Tusty's entrepreneurial effort, dedication, skill, and incredibly hard work.

I thank also the genuinely wonderful staff at Greenleaf Book Group, especially Aaron Hierholzer and Bill Crawford. Aaron's and Bill's enthusiasm for the book, and their unfailingly hard work made the production of this little volume, for me, a real joy.

Other friends to whom I am hopelessly in intellectual and professional debt are too numerous to name—but I'll nevertheless name a few of them, aware that I'll forget many who will then justifiably be miffed at me for not listing them here. So I thank, from the bottom of my heart:

Karol and Thomas above all.

My colleague and co-blogger Russ Roberts, who has taught me so much about economics and about writing—as have my colleagues Walter Williams, Jim Bennett, Pete Boettke, Bryan Caplan, Tyler Cowen, Tom Hazlett, Dan Klein, Alex Tabarrok, Dick Wagner, and Larry White.

Each and every one of my other George Mason University colleagues in Economics and in the Law School, whose scholarship and learning inspire me daily.

My current and former students—who are always the single best source of penetrating questions and feedback.

My former GMU students Liya Palagashvili and Laura Sacher who helped so expertly to prepare the graphs that accompany several of the letters.

John Stossel, who inspired me to (try to) be more creative in expressing myself to audiences of non-economists.

Ditto for Sheldon Richman of the Foundation for Economic Education.

Betsy and Lyle Albaugh, Sarah and Paul Atkins, Christine and John Blundell, Andrea and Shannon Boudreaux, Ruth and Ryan Boudreaux, Katya and Kevin Brancato, Mary and Joel Centanni, Laura and Jim Clancy, Kristina and Ed Crane, Liz and Steve Davies, Helen and Prentiss Davis, Jeanine and Fred Dent, Rebecca and Bill Dunn, Hans Eicholz, Anita and Burt Folsom, Nancy and Ed Grass, Elizabeth and Bob Higgs, Lora and Randy Holcombe, Candace and Vernon Smith, Fran and Fred Smith, Dot and Bruce Yandle, as well as June Arunga, Jim Blasingame, David Boaz, Reuvain Borchardt, Jack Censer, Carrie Conko, Mike Cox, Wayne Crews, Vero de Rugy, Jim Dorn, Kerry Dugas, Bob Ekelund, Ken Elzinga, Bill Field, Darryl Fontaine, David Fontaine, Pierre Garello, Roger Garrison, Nick Gillespie, Walter Grinder, Dan Griswold, David Henderson, Brian Hooks, Sandy Ikeda, Dan Ikenson, Jeff Jacoby, Sallie James, Kristi Kendall, Arnold Kling, Roger Koppl, Dwight Lee, Leonard Liggio, Tibor Machan, Henry Manne, Michelle McAdoo, Fred McChesney, Deirdre McCloskey, Roger Meiners, Andy Morriss, Victor Niederhoffer, Mary Anastasia O'Grady, Tom Palmer, John Papola, Mark Perry, Adam Pritchard, Greg Rehmke, David Rose, Alan Russell, Andy Rutten, Nick Schulz, George Selgin, Amity Shlaes, Roger Silk, Kathy Spolarich, Daniele Struppa, Joe Swanson, Mark Thornton, John Tierney, Bob Tollison, Oscar Varela, Eric Wanner, Fred Young, Ryan Young, Marty Zupan, Todd Zywicki, and Many Others Who I Know I'm Forgetting.

Each of these folks, not all of whom share my perspective, contributed in some positive way to my "letters" and, hence, to this book.

Thanks to you all.

July 2012
Fairfax, VA

Free To Choose Press is grateful to the following patrons, without whom this book would not have been possible.

Ed Barr
Dunn's Foundation for the Advancement of Right Thinking
J. P. Humphreys Foundation
Lou Carabini
Rick Wolf
Barry Conner
Gerry Ohrstrom
Randy Kendrick
Victor Niederhoffer

★ ★ ★

"Freedom is hammered out
on the anvil of discussion,
dissent, and debate."

—Hubert Humphrey

I DON'T WANT TO BE UNIFIED.

....

14 October 2007

The Editor, New York Times
620 Eighth Avenue
New York, NY 10018

To the Editor:

Thomas Friedman wants "a president who can unify the country around meaningful action on energy and climate" ("Who Will Succeed Al Gore?" October 14).

I get the creeps whenever I encounter anyone seeking national "unity." A practical impossibility in a nation of 300 million people, "unifying the country" really means government seizing enormous amounts of additional power in order to embark upon schemes of social engineering—schemes whose pursuit gratifies the abstract fantasies of the theory class and, simultaneously, lines the very real pockets of politically powerful corporations, organizations, and "experts."

I want a president who will stick exclusively to protecting my freedoms.

Sincerely,

Kids naturally want to save the planet—just like they naturally want to clean up their rooms.

THE ABSURDITY OF SUCH A NOTION IS DIFFICULT TO COMPREHEND.

25 April 2010

Editor, The New York Times
620 Eighth Avenue
New York, NY 10018

To the Editor:

The group Green My Parents teaches children to prod adults into becoming more 'green' ("How to Green Your Parents," April 22). Allison Arieff approves. She croons that "GMP recognizes that young people are inherently attuned to their environment and understand the importance of protecting it."

Please.

Kids aren't inherently attuned to the environmental condition of even their own bedrooms, as a peek into a typical twelve-year-old's room will instantly prove. So it's asinine to think that children "inherently" care about the condition of Siberia or of Brazilian rainforests.

Today's prattling by young people about how awfully dirty the globe is reflects not kids' "inherent" tuning-in to the global environment but, instead, their indoctrination—performed by teachers and popular media—into the Church of Gaia.

Sincerely,

★ ★ ★

"The powers not delegated
to the United States by the
Constitution,
nor prohibited by it to the
States, are reserved to the States
respectively, or to the people."

—Amendment 10: Powers of the States and
People, Ratified December 15, 1791

ART. I, SEC. 8 DOES NOT READ: "CONGRESS SHALL HAVE POWER THE TO MAKE ALL LAWS THAT IT DEEMS WILL BE GOOD FOR THE PEOPLE."

5 July 2010

Editor, USA Today
7950 Jones Branch Drive
McLean, VA 22108-0605

Dear Editor:

Sandra Day O'Connor and George Nethercutt are correct that too many Americans lack sufficient understanding of U.S. history and of the meaning of this nation's founding documents ("Celebrate America by learning about her," July 3). In no group of Americans does this ignorance run more deeply and malignantly than it does for those in Congress and in the White House.

Aimed at ensuring that there would be no misunderstanding, the Tenth amendment makes clear what James Madison wrote in Federalist Paper #45 about the U.S. Constitution: "The powers delegated by the proposed Constitution to the Federal Government are few and defined." Those few powers are enumerated and defined in Article I, Section 8. Read the 429 words of this part of the Constitution and you'll find no authority there (or anywhere else in the Constitution) for Uncle Sam to enforce minimum wages; to command Americans to purchase health insurance; to dictate the hiring practices of private firms; to operate a universal 'pension' program; to oversee or fund education; to subsidize farmers—indeed, no authority to do so much of what Washington does today as a matter of routine.

Yet every elected official in America swears an oath to uphold the Constitution. Clearly, these oaths are muttered insincerely or in inexcusable ignorance (or both).

Sincerely,

11

It's up to Mark Twain, and not Michael Walker, whether he wishes to post online for free.

AND, HEY, NO PUBLICATION PAYS FOR PUBLISHED LETTERS TO THE EDITOR.

1 April 2011

Editor, Los Angeles Times
202 West 1st Street
Los Angeles, California 90012

Dear Editor:

I'm in the odd position of agreeing with the Huffington Post. Michael Walker criticizes that popular on-line publication for its policy of not paying $$$ to its contributors ("Why should writers work for no pay?" April 1). Arianna Huffington replies that the abundant exposure that the site she founded (and now owned by AOL) provides to aspiring pundits is itself sufficient compensation.

Ms. Huffington is unquestionably correct. Because her site is only one of thousands of venues to which pundits can peddle their prose, and because many lesser-known pundits continue to eagerly write for the HP without expecting money from the HP, the HP clearly provides ample value to its contributing writers. Tit for tat. Voluntary trade with mutual benefits. All parties to the transactions gain and no one loses. Works out nicely; it truly does.

A lesson here that I hope Ms. Huffington and her colleagues will take to heart is that third parties, even when well-intentioned, are poorly positioned to assess the merits of—and to second-guess the detailed terms of—capitalist acts among consenting adults.

Sincerely,

Americans produce cars here by growing corn, shipping it to Japan, and receiving cars in return.

MORICI SEEMINGLY IS UNAWARE OF DAVID FRIEDMAN'S DISCOVERY THAT IOWANS GROW CARS IN THEIR CORNFIELDS.

6 November 2011

Editor, FoxNews.com
1211 Avenue of the Americas
New York, NY 10036

Dear Editor:

Peter Morici claims that a trade deficit is "lost purchasing power" ("What's Holding Back Job Creation," Nov. 4). He's hopelessly confused.

Evidence of this confusion abounds. In the middle of his op-ed Prof. Morici laments businesses' "[i]nadequate investment in labor saving technology," yet he ends his op-ed by complaining that foreigners (especially the Chinese) ship too many goods to us in exchange for what we ship to them.

Say what? Because labor-saving technology is indeed good, then trading arrangements that enable us Americans to get more imports for fewer exports are also good. If, say, American electronics producers would demand two hours of my economics lectures in exchange for one of their flat-screen TVs, while foreign producers demand only one hour of my lectures, I save labor by purchasing the foreign-made TV. That is, I'm made richer by buying my TV from abroad. (And I'll be made even richer if tomorrow the foreign producer lowers the price of its TV to only 30 minutes of my lecturing.)

Trade itself is a labor-saving technology, to be applauded no less enthusiastically than we applaud mechanization and other labor-saving technologies.

Sincerely,

15

You too can become an energy expert.

THE ARROGANCE OF THESE PEOPLE NEVER CEASES TO AMAZE.

....

13 May 2010

Editor, USA Today
7950 Jones Branch Drive
McLean, VA 22108-0605

Dear Editor:

Sen. Bill Nelson claims that "The ultimate answer to America's energy needs lies not in oil, but in the rapid development of alternative fuels" ("Halt offshore exploration," May 13).

How in the world does Mr. Nelson divine this alleged fact? Does he have expert insight into the full costs and benefits of developing and producing non-fossil fuels? Has he displayed a unique talent at predicting changes in the technologies that are used to extract petroleum? Hardly.

After a short stint in the Army, Mr. Nelson spent all of one year (1970) in the private sector (where he practiced law). From 1971 until today he has worked exclusively in politics. He has neither experience in the energy industry nor any record of entrepreneurship. For nearly 40 years—well over half of his life—he's devoted his career to spending other people's money. In short, he has no basis for making this claim.

Mr. Nelson's "answer to America's energy needs" deserves no more attention than does any such prophecy issued by a Ouija board or by a witch doctor reading the entrails of a rooster.

Sincerely,

[signature]

"My looks got me this job."

LIKE TOO MANY LAW PROFESSORS TODAY, DEBORAH RHODE MISTAKENLY THINKS THAT "LAW" MEANS "COMMAND." PERHAPS HER EMPLOYER SHOULD CHANGE ITS NAME TO STANFORD COMMAND SCHOOL—AN INSTITUTION THAT TRAINS ITS STUDENTS IN THE SCIENCE OF ORDERING OTHERS ABOUT.

10 June 2010

Editor, Los Angeles Times
202 West 1st Street
Los Angeles, California 90012

Dear Editor:

Meghan Daum reports that Stanford law professor Deborah Rhode wants legislation to prevent "lookism" ("Business: beastly toward beauty?" June 10). Ms. Rhode is disturbed that human beings prefer attractive people to unattractive people, and she wants to stop us—or at least stop business people, who channel their customers' preferences—from acting on this preference.

Ms. Rhode's proposal reminds me of Kurt Vonnegut's 1961 short story, "Harrison Bergeron,"[1] about a dystopia in which government intrudes obscenely into everyone's lives in order to achieve total equality of outcomes. Implants are put into smart people's brains to disrupt their better-than-average abilities to reason; "handicap bags" are worn by strong people to consume their above-average strengths; and masks are clamped over the faces of attractive people to hide their beauty.

While Ms. Rhode's proposal doesn't yet go this far, it shares the same totalitarian spirit that Vonnegut warned against. Those consumed with this spirit regard an imperfection in society—unequal abilities and opportunities—as an evil whose elimination justifies not only the most oppressive restrictions on people's freedoms but also the most tyrannical suppression of their very thoughts and desires.

Sincerely,

Donald J. Boudreaux

Segregated drinking fountains in the Dougherty County Courthouse,
Albany, Georgia. Brought to you by government.

JIM CROW WAS LEGISLATION.

22 May 2010

Editor, The New York Times
620 Eighth Avenue
New York, NY 10018

To the Editor:

Reacting to Rand Paul's remarks about the 1964 Civil Rights Act, you say that his libertarian philosophy "is a theory of liberty with roots in America's creation, but the succeeding centuries have shown how ineffective it was in promoting a civil society . . . It was only government power that . . . abolished Jim Crow" ("Limits of Libertarianism," May 22).

You've got it backwards. Jim Crow itself was government power. Jim Crow was legislation that forced the segregation of blacks from whites. Research shows that people acting in the free market that you apparently believe is prone to racial discrimination were remarkably reluctant to discriminate along racial lines. It was this very reluctance—this capacity of free markets to make people colorblind—that obliged racists in the late 19th century to use government to achieve their loathsome goals.[1]

Had Mr. Rand's libertarian philosophy been followed more consistently throughout American history, there would have been no need for one government statute (the Civil Rights Act) to upend earlier government statutes (Jim Crow) and the business practices that they facilitated.

Sincerely,

Market opportunities, not special ops, distinguish America from other civilizations.

WESTERN EXCEPTIONALISM.

4 May 2011

Editor, The Wall Street Journal
1211 6th Ave.
New York, NY 10036

Dear Editor:

I disagree with Holman Jenkins's thesis that the killing of Osama bin Laden "vindicates" American civilization ("Civilization Vindicated," May 4). However necessary or just it was to kill Bin Laden, a civilization's value is never measured by the skill with which its government kills even the most deserving victims.

Governments have killed people for millennia. In taking down Bin Laden, the U.S. government simply did what governments throughout the ages have regularly done.

What distinguishes America and the west from most other civilizations (including the primitive one championed by Bin Laden) isn't our skill at martial deeds, but our embrace of individual liberty—liberty that clears space for peaceful and creative commerce. Our civilization is vindicated by our supermarkets full of food, by our shopping malls full of clothing, by our homes with solid floors and solid roofs and automatic dishwashers, by iPads and aspirin and antibiotics and Amazon.com, by the globe-spanning cooperation that makes all of these things real—and by the freedom from central direction and mind-numbing, soul-shriveling superstitions that have made so many other 'civilizations' sanguinary and hellish.

Sincerely,

Donald J Boudreaux

"If goods don't cross borders, soldiers will."

—attributed to Frederic Bastiat (1801–1850)

WITH THANKS TO MY BETTER HALF FOR THIS INSIGHT.

· ·

7 December 2006

The Editor, The New Yorker
4 Times Square
New York, NY 10036

To the Editor:

Lou Dobbs believes "unequivocally" that free trade harms ordinary Americans ("Mad as Hell," Dec. 4). So being a courageous man of principle, he'll no doubt soon inform his bosses at Time-Warner, CNN's owner, that they contribute to the demise of middle-class America by broadcasting (according to CNN's website) in "Asia Pacific, South Asia, Europe, Middle East, Japan, Africa, Latin America, North America." And when his bosses refuse to stop trading internationally, I await hearing Mr. Dobbs thunder on air that CNN's participation in globalization is yet another instance of shameless corporate greed.

Sincerely,

"I was just negotiating our fair share of taxes with the IRS agent."

A NATION WITH A SUFFICIENT NUMBER OF SUCH SHEEP WILL SURELY HEAD FOR SLAUGHTER.

17 December 2010

Editor, The New York Times
620 Eighth Avenue
New York, NY 10018

To the Editor:

Reproaching people who complain about taxes, Liane Norman insists that "taxes are really just prices" (Letters, Dec. 17).

No ma'am. Prices are terms of exchanges voluntarily agreed to by willing buyers and willing sellers. Because prices result from people spending—or not spending!—their own money, they reflect genuine consumer desires and resource scarcities.

In stark contrast, taxes are forced extractions. Even when spent with the intent of benefitting taxpayers, taxes—unlike prices—are never the result of bargains between buyers and sellers. Taxes, instead, are the result of commands issued by rulers to subjects.

Buyers who refuse to pay sellers' asking prices go without the goods. Subjects who refuse to pay the sovereign's demanded tax go to jail.

Sincerely,

Donald J. Boudreaux

By permission of Chip Bok and Creators Syndicate, Inc.

We were denied permission to reproduce the *New Yorker* cover in this book, but you can find the image online at the artist's website: www.bobstaake.com/nyer/reflection.shtml.

THE MESSIAH-NIZATION CONTINUES.
....

13 November 2008

Editor, The New Yorker
4 Times Square
New York, NY 10036

Dear Editor:

Your November 17th cover shows the "O" in "New Yorker" as an Obama "O", rising like a radiant and beneficent moon into a peaceful night sky.

This picture is beautiful. It's also terrifying.

Even to hint that any human being possesses super-human powers—that he or she is anointed by celestial forces—that he or she reigns over the rest of us in some grander-than-human fashion—is an atavistic reflex, one that modern humanity should have progressed beyond.

Americans rightly laugh at the ridiculous things that many North Koreans believe (or are at least told) about Kim Jong-il. Let us not turn ourselves into objects of similar ridicule.

Sincerely,

[signature]

,,BOSTON TEA-PARTY."
Three cargoes of tea des-
troyed. Dec. 16. 1773.

A number of the inhabitants,
disguised as Indians, boarded
the ships in the night, broke
open all the chests of tea,
and emptied the contents
into the sea.

Did the participants in the original Tea Party have a "fatuous infatuation" with liberty?

AND IT'S NOT EVEN AN INFATUATION
THAT'S SOBER AND MATURE . . .

21 September 2010

Editor, Washington Post
1150 15th St., NW
Washington, DC 20071

Dear Editor:

Enjoying an uproariously good time poking fun at the Tea Party, Richard Cohen helpfully explains that its adherents' insistence on strict interpretation of the Constitution is the result of a "fatuous infatuation" with that document—is the consequence of a yokel-like refusal to recognize that the Constitution is valuable "only because it has been wisely adapted to changing times. To adhere to the very word of its every clause hardly is respectful to the Founding Fathers" ("Republicans under a spell," Sept. 21).

Question for Mr. Cohen: if government officials and the courts are free to choose which words of the Constitution to "adhere to" and which to ignore, what meaning does the Constitution really possess? And why did the Founding Fathers struggle so hard during the long, hot summer of 1787 over the precise wording of the Constitution? Why didn't they—to ensure that they would win the respect of future generations of Very Smart Persons—simply draft a document that reads "Government may do whatever it judges to be best for The People" and leave it at that?

Sincerely,

Donald Boudreaux

Free societies build bridges, not walls.

29 August 2007

Editor, USA Today
7950 Jones Branch Drive
McLean, VA 22108-0605

To the Editor:

The Internet, cell phones, GPS navigation, and the Boston Red Sox's
2004 World Series victory are just some of the happy marvels of the
past quarter-century. Alas, 2007 differs from 1982 also in ways less
happy—one of which is the re-emergence of xenophobia. 9/11 fueled
this ugly trend. But even before that awful September day Americans
were growing more overtly hostile to immigrants. Groundless fears over
jobs and threats to America's culture are stoked successfully today by
nativist rabble-rousers such as Lou Dobbs and Michelle Malkin. Modern "Minutemen" officiously "guard" Americans against immigrants. A
700-mile-long wall is being built to "protect" us from Latin Americans
seeking work. Across the land there spreads a disquieting "us-versus-
them" mentality.

Take note, though: All great societies are open societies. They fear neither competition nor different cultures. They are stimulated by con-
trasts and they welcome new perspectives. They are optimistic, tolerant,
confident, and, as a result, dynamic, strong, and prosperous. They avoid
the stupidity of tribalism.

My fervent hope is that by 2032 Americans will have rejected once and
for all the ignorant intolerance of today's bigoted, big-mouthed, and
benighted xenophobes.

Sincerely,

Donald J Boudreaux

The term *free lunch* originally referred to free food offered by American saloon keepers to attract drinkers into their establishments. This advertisement for a Milwaukee saloon appeared in the *Commercial Advertiser* in June 1850:

At The Crescent . . .

Can be found the choicest of Segars, Wines and Liquors. . .

N. B.—A free lunch every day at 11 o'clock will be served up.

If you purchased drinks, you got a free lunch. In addition to being criticized by the temperance lobby, many pointed out that the lunches weren't "free" but were paid for by the customer in the price of the drinks they had to buy—the same point behind the twentieth-century economic concept of "There ain't no such thing as a free lunch."

In fact, according to www.phrases.org.uk, some saloon owners were charged with false advertising, since customers couldn't get the "free" lunch without turning over money first, even if it was for drinks.[2]

REALITY AIN'T OPTIONAL: THERE'S NO FREE LUNCH, OR FREE HEALTH CARE.

••

21 January 2010

Editor, Los Angeles Times
202 West 1st Street
Los Angeles, California 90012

Dear Editor:

Hoping for the electoral defeat of members of Congress who vote against Obamacare, Don Warner asks your readers to think of these Obamacare opponents "Every time you have to pay an extravagant co-pay, every time you must make up a huge deductible" (Letters, Jan. 21).

In other words, Mr. Warner asks me to be angry whenever I actually have to pay for resources that I use—to be peeved that someone else isn't footing my bill—to be upset that Uncle Sam hasn't arranged for me to free-ride on other people's nickels—to strike back at politicians who refuse to force Mr. Warner to pay my health-care expenses and me to pay his.

I reject Mr. Warner's childish advice and his predatory principles.

Sincerely,

Otto von Bismarck, father of the Welfare State

HOWE WE'VE PROGRESSED BEYOND THAT PETTY 18TH-CENTURY NOTION OF INDIVIDUAL RIGHTS.

22 February 2010

Editor, Washington Post
1150 15th St., NW
Washington, DC 20071

Dear Editor:

Robert Samuelson observes that "Every advanced society, including the United States, has a welfare state. Though details differ, their purposes are similar: to support the unemployed, poor, disabled and aged" ("Greece and the welfare state in ruins," Feb. 22). True, but incomplete.

The founder of the modern welfare state, German Chancellor Otto von Bismarck, wanted, as he said, "to bribe the working classes" into devotion to the German state. What better way to ensure that families are willing to send ample supplies of their young men off to die for the Fatherland?

And it's telling that an American admirer of this German system, Frederic C. Howe—who was influential in planting these "progressive" ideas in America's upper Midwest—admitted that one result of government-dispensed welfare is that "The individual exists for the state, not the state for the individual."[3]

If Mr. Samuelson is correct that welfare 'entitlements' now threaten to bankrupt governments around the globe, we persons whose puny individual needs are nothing as compared to those of the state had better beware.

Sincerely,

Donald J. Boudreaux

Putting out raging fires—like defending our country—is not a job for the coerced.

THE FETISH FOR FORCE IS PECULIARLY WIDESPREAD.

....

6 December 2009

Editor, Boston Globe
P.O. Box 55819
Boston, MA 02205-5819

Dear Editor:

Barry Brodsky asserts that military conscription is "just and honorable" (Letters, Dec. 6).

Really? Forcing young men and women to fight against their will is "just"? Confiscating several years of their lives by coercing them to serve the state is "honorable"?

Also, is it really "political cowardice" to reject a system in which people are rounded up and impressed into "service"?

More questions: Does Mr. Brodsky think it unjust and dishonorable that firefighting and policing are performed only by persons who choose to enter these professions? And does he suppose that the quality of fire-fighting and policing would improve if these tasks were entrusted to persons who must be coerced into performing them?

Sincerely,

Donald J. Boudreaux

The Caricaturist's Apology

"You Rascal! I dare to say this is not like me and I'll make you eat it."
Imagine the caricaturist of 1802 having to abide by a fairness doctrine . . .

HOW ABOUT A FREEDOM DOCTRINE?

19 June 2009

Editor, Los Angeles Times
202 West 1st Street
Los Angeles, California 90012

Dear Editor:

Seth Hill writes that "Every time I'm surfing channels and I happen by mistake to land there [on the Fox News channel], I have to watch a commentary by [Newt] Gingrich or former Vice President Dick Cheney. That channel makes me long for the days of the Fairness Doctrine" (Letters, June 19).

Mr. Hill's attitude is the seed of totalitarianism: unable to distinguish what he does voluntarily from what he is coerced into doing, he wants to use force to save himself from the annoyance of fleetingly encountering disagreeable ideas as he flips his channel changer—and to use force to hamper other persons' access to those ideas.

There's nothing fair about that.

Sincerely,

Galveston Disaster,   A slightly twisted house.

Y-IKES!

··············

16 September 2008

News Editor, WAMU Radio
Brandywine Building
4400 Massachusetts Avenue, NW
Washington, DC 20016-8082

Dear Sir or Madam:

This morning your reporter interviewed a resident of Galveston, Texas, about the effects of hurricane Ike. The person interviewed said that she went to the gasoline station before Ike hit to "top off" her tank. But she was angry to find that gasoline prices had jumped 50 cents per gallon from the day before. "It's ridiculous," this woman opined. "Ike hadn't hit yet!"

Your reporter should have immediately asked this woman: "Well, why were you topping off your tank? Ike hadn't hit yet."

Gasoline became more scarce—more precious—in Galveston the moment Ike's arrival became imminent. Gasoline retailers acted in anticipation of the future no more or no less than did motorists, such as your interviewee, who topped off their tanks.

Sincerely,

Donald J. Boudreaux

★ ★ ★

Capitalist's motto:
"I want what I earn."

Socialist's motto:
"I want what you earn."

"I WANT TO KEEP WHAT I EARN" IS REGARDED AS GREEDY AND UNENLIGHTENED.

"I WANT TO KEEP WHAT YOU EARN" IS REGARDED AS SELFLESS AND PROGRESSIVE.

BIZARRE.

....

9 July 2009

Editor, Washington Post
1150 15th St., NW
Washington, DC 20071

Dear Editor:

E.J. Dionne describes capitalism as "a system rooted in materialist values" ("To the Right of the Pope," July 9). "Materialist values" is a vague term, but if—as seems to be the case—Mr. Dionne thinks the chief justification for capitalism is that it generates lots of stuff for consumers, he's mistaken.

While capitalism empathically does improve material living standards, all the great champions of economic freedom (aka capitalism) ultimately justify this system because only it affords true dignity to individuals—the dignity that is denied by interventionist systems which arbitrarily diminish each person's freedom to choose. For "Progressives" such as Mr. Dionne not to share the value of freedom is fine. But it's rather cheeky to accuse, with one breath, proponents of capitalism of being unduly focused on material goods, and with the next breath to insist that a major problem with capitalism is that some people get fewer material goods than do other people.

Sincerely,

[signature]

Mao Zedong's "Great Leap Forward" was intended to rapidly transform the People's Republic of China from an agrarian economy into a modern communist nation. Mao led the movement based on his "Theory of Productive Forces." Sounds good, doesn't it?

The campaign was a disaster, ultimately causing tens of millions of deaths. In his book *Mao's Great Famine*, historian Frank Dikötter writes that "coercion, terror, and systematic violence were the foundation of the Great Leap Forward" and notes that from 15 to 32 million lives were the price of this wonderfully named government program.

THE FOLLOWING IS PROPOSED WITH ONLY HALF OF MY TONGUE IN MY CHEEK.

16 June 2010

Editor, Washington Post
1150 15th St., NW
Washington, DC 20071

Dear Editor:

Sens. John Kerry and Joe Lieberman propose the "American Power Act" to, as you report, "tax carbon dioxide emissions produced by coal-fired power plants and other large polluters" ("Climate bill faces long odds, despite Obama speech," June 16).

Hmmm. Because it's unclear how taxing major sources of power will promote American power, this bill's title is misleading. Pondering this fact reveals that too many statutes are known only by the happy clichés serving as their titles—for example, the "No Child Left Behind Act."

Such titling of legislation is dangerous. Proponents of, say, the "Patriot Act" can too easily portray all opponents as being unpatriotically hostile to mom, apple pie, and all else American.

So I propose my own statute: the "No Legislation Has a Title" act. This statute would prohibit government employees from publicly referring to any bill or statute in ways other than by a number assigned to that statute. For instance, Sens. Kerry's and Lieberman's bill might be assigned the number 9—in which case that bill would forevermore be called simply "Act 9."

Stripping legislation of titles would oblige each statute's supporters to articulate details of how the statute will operate. And citizens would be more likely to investigate each statute's contents rather than merely assume that statutes will achieve the goals announced by disingenuous titles.

Sincerely,

[signature]

A valuable product or costly future landfill? The market has to decide.

PAPER HYPOCRISY.

18 August 2009

Editor, Concord Monitor
One Monitor Drive
P.O. Box 1177
Concord, New Hampshire 03302-1177

Dear Editor:

Asserting that "habitual consumption of bottled water is a waste of money" (Isn't that for each consumer of bottled water to determine?) you criticize bottled water as being a "source of landfill waste. An estimated 60 million plastic bottles are dumped in landfills every day." You further allege that "drinking bottled water also wastes fuel" ("Americans don't need Fiji's water," August 17).

Let me try my hand at such arrogance:

Habitual reading of newspapers is a waste of money. Newspapers are a source of landfill waste. Millions of tons of newsprint are dumped into landfills every day. And producing these inky pages also wastes fuel—fuel used to power paper mills, printing presses, and delivery trucks. Oh, and what about trees?! How many trees are cut down each year simply to gratify the self-indulgent desire of consumers to read newspapers and the greedy itch of publishers to reap profits?

Now realizing what a scourge you are to your readers and to the environment, will you shut down? And if not, why not? Can you explain how producing and reading newspapers differs from producing and drinking bottled water?

Sincerely,

Donald Boudreaux

Only expensive goods for sale here

A DIFFERENT TAKE.

3 May 2011

Editor, The Wall Street Journal
1211 6th Ave.
New York, NY 10036

Dear Editor:

Peter Donovan asserts that failure of government to subsidize loans to build lower-end rental units would result in poor Americans being homeless (Letters, May 3).

Nonsense. Unsubsidized markets do not cater exclusively to the middle-income and rich. Quite the contrary. Automakers produce not only luxury vehicles such as Lexuses but larger numbers of low-end makes such as Chevys (not to mention the existence of a thriving market in used cars). We see not only high-end retailers selling the likes of hand-crafted Stickley furniture but also, and more abundantly, Wal-Mart and other discount retailers selling inexpensive household furnishings. America boasts not only pricey restaurants such as the Inn at Little Washington but, far more commonly, inexpensive eateries such as Olive Garden, Denny's, and (dare I mention it?) McDonald's.

This same pattern holds for clothing, hotels, groceries, entertainment, works of art, and nearly every other species of goods and services in our economy. It's unreasonable to suppose that without government-subsidized loans to developers, housing would be built only for middle-income and rich Americans.

Sincerely,

Donald J. Boudreaux

When considering the economic impact of transporting goods, vehicle
size matters.

SEEN AND UNSEEN.

·······························

4 June 2010

News Editor, WTOP Radio
3400 Idaho Avenue, NW
Washington, DC 20016

Dear Sir or Madam:

I missed the name of the expert interviewed today, during the 11am hour, who said that farmers' markets are better for the environment than are supermarkets because foods sold at farmers' markets "are shipped shorter distances" than are foods sold at supermarkets.

This expert jumps too quickly to what is probably a mistaken conclusion.

Although foods sold at farmers' markets are indeed grown close to the places where they are sold, these foods are also transported from farm to market in small vehicles—typically, in pick-up trucks. In contrast, foods sold in supermarkets are generally shipped from farm to market in very large vehicles, each of which moves to market multiple times more foods than is moved by pick-up trucks. Therefore, the amount of carbon used to transport, say, each tomato and each link of artisan sausage to a supermarket is likely *less* than is the amount of carbon emitted to transport each of these items to a farmers' market.

Sincerely,

Donald J Boudreaux

Adam Smith L.L.D.

Adam Smith is the author of *Wealth of Nations*, which sought to reveal the nature and causes of a nation's prosperity.

Someone earning money by his own labor benefits himself. Unknowingly, he also benefits society, because to earn income on his labor in a competitive market, he must produce something others value. In Adam Smith's lasting imagery, "By directing that industry in such a manner as its produce may be of greatest value, he intends only his own gain, and he is in this, as in many other cases, led by an invisible hand to promote an end which was no part of his intention."

Smith saw the main cause of prosperity as increasing division of labor.[4]

"WHAT HAS ALWAYS MADE A HELL ON EARTH HAS BEEN THAT MAN HAS TRIED TO MAKE IT HIS HEAVEN." —FRIEDRICH HOLDERIN

....

31 May 2007

Editor, Washington Post
1150 15th St., NW
Washington, DC 20071

Dear Editor:

George Will's eloquent "Case for Conservatism" (May 31) really is the case for liberalism—the liberalism of Adam Smith, Turgot, Madison, Mencken, and Hayek. This true liberalism has at its core a genuine respect for individual autonomy. It rejects as a dangerous delusion the belief in salvation by Great Leaders or Big Plans. True liberals understand that great societies are not constructed according to blueprints. They understand also that our world can never be perfect and that attempts to create heaven on earth inevitably produce hell.

Sincerely,

★ ★ ★

"Hell isn't merely paved with good intentions; it's walled and roofed with them. Yes, and furnished too."

—Aldous Huxley

BAD ECONOMICS.

. . . .

13 November 2009

Editor, The New York Times
620 Eighth Avenue
New York, NY 10018

To the Editor:

To combat unemployment, Paul Krugman supports "labor rules that discourage firing" ("Free to Lose," Nov. 13). If a student in my Principles of Economics course ever wrote such a thing on an exam, he or she would earn an F.

But no student in my class would ever write such nonsense. My students learn from day one to distinguish intentions from results. So my students understand that the intention of such labor rules might be to decrease unemployment, but that the result will be to increase it— because my students also understand that labor rules that discourage firing raise employers' costs of hiring workers to begin with. Firms will think twice—thrice!—before hiring employees who, once on the job, are difficult to fire.

If the goal is to decrease unemployment, raising firms' costs of hiring unemployed workers is emphatically counterproductive.

Sincerely,

Budget Deficit as a Percentage of GDP in 2005 & 2009

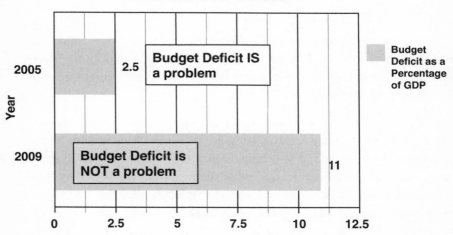

Data compiled from budget figures available from the White House Office of Management and Budget: http://www.whitehouse.gov/omb/budget/Historicals

DEFICIENT PERSPECTIVE.

....

28 August 2009

Editor, The New York Times
620 Eighth Avenue
New York, NY 10018

To the Editor:

Noting that "it's important to have some perspective," Paul Krugman argues that while Uncle Sam's budget deficit is now large, "we also have a huge economy, which means that things aren't as scary as you might think" ("Till Debt Does Its Part," August 28). Whew! No cause for much concern, for the size of America's GDP swamps the size of the budget deficit.

During the Bush years, however, Mr. Krugman preached a different gospel. For example, in his February 11, 2005 column—devoted to condemning tax cuts—he insisted that "the deficit is indeed a major problem."

So let's take Mr. Krugman's advice and get some perspective. In 2005, when Mr. Krugman insisted that government's budget deficit was "indeed a major problem," that deficit was 2.5 percent of GDP. Today, when Mr. Krugman no longer is very concerned about the budget deficit, that deficit will be about 11 percent of GDP. Hmmmm . . .

Sincerely,

AND IN THE PRIVACY OF HIS OWN MIND, WALTER MITTY WAS REALLY A REMARKABLE ADVENTURER!

••

8 February 2007

The Editor, New York Times
229 West 43rd St.
New York, NY 10036

To the Editor:

David Brooks vividly explains that today's politicians, who are often sensible in private, camoflauge themselves in public: they routinely endorse policies that they really don't believe in ("Private Virtue, Public Vice," Feb. 8). Then Brooks strangely concludes "In private, we have a decent leadership class. In public, it's rotten."

Persons who are wise and steadfast only in private—only when they suffer no risks for sticking to their principles—are neither decent nor leaders. They are opportunists, poseurs, and rogues.

Sincerely,

Further Conclusions from Polachek and Seiglie

"The proposition that international trade specifically, and economic interdependence in general reduces conflict between nations has a long tradition in the history of economic thought. The argument proposed is that trade leads to welfare gains that countries do not want to jeopardize losing by engaging in trade-disruptive activities such as wars or other forms of conflict. Yet, until fairly recent times economists have not applied some of the modern tools of economics to explore this proposition. This is surprising given the large cost to society of diverting resources towards a purely predatory or redistributive motive instead of productive activity. Given the slow pace of economic development in large parts of the world ravaged by conflict, and the dim prospects of a convergence of their income with those of the developed world, it seems the incentives to explore this topic is of some urgency."

FREE TRADE AND PEACE.

• •

13 May 2008

Editor, The Wall Street Journal
200 Liberty Street
New York, NY 10281

To the Editor:

Mark Helprin correctly points out that as the Chinese grow more prosperous their military will grow more mighty ("The Challenge From
China," May 13). He advises that Uncle Sam dramatically increase the
size of his own arsenal.

Regardless of this suggestion's merits or demerits, the more vital course
is for Uncle Sam to immediately eliminate all trade and investment
restrictions with China, and for politicians to stop threatening further
restrictions. Such moves would speed the integration of China's economy with our own. Being economically integrated means being economically reliant on each other—a happy recipe for prosperity and peace.

Want evidence? See the important work of economists Solomon
Polachek and Carlos Seiglie. Their empirical research leads them to
conclude that "international cooperation in reducing barriers to both
trade and capital flows can promote a more peaceful world."[5] Want
more evidence? Ask yourself how likely are even a well-armed Canada
or Japan to have any interest in shooting their countless customers and
suppliers throughout the U.S.? The answer, of course, is no more likely
than we are to want to shoot our customers and suppliers throughout
those countries.

Sincerely,

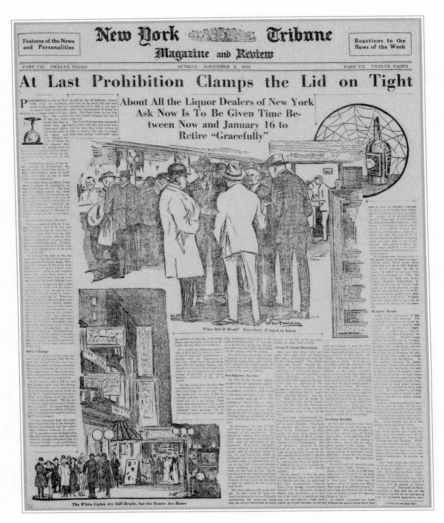

When prohibited, alcohol was controlled by Al Capone, Bugsy Siegel, and other mobsters. Legalized alcohol is controlled by Anheuser-Busch, MillerCoors, and other legal corporations.

WHAT ARE THEY SMOKING?

···

25 August 2010

Editor, Los Angeles Times
202 West 1st Street
Los Angeles, California 90012

Dear Editor:

Arguing against Proposition 19—the passage of which would liberalize marijuana laws in California—former U.S. "Drug Czars" Gil Kerlikowske, John Walters, Barry McCaffrey, Lee Brown, Bob Martinez, and William Bennett assert that "No country in the world has legalized marijuana to the extent envisioned by Proposition 19" ("Why California should just say no to Prop. 19," August 25).

Not true. Marijuana was perfectly legal throughout the United States until the city of El Paso first outlawed it in 1914, a move that was followed in the same year by national criminalization with the Harrison Act.

The long historical record of legal marijuana in America—a record dating from the 17th century until the lifetimes of many people still alive today—offers no support for the authors' contention that liberalized marijuana laws will result in a slew of terrible problems.

Sincerely,

★ ★ ★

"The reformers' preferred metaphor is 'leveling the playing field.' They should listen to the logic of their language: fields are leveled by bulldozers."

—George F. Will

KEEP SPEECH FREE.
....

9 June 2010

Editor, The New York Times
620 Eighth Avenue
New York, NY 10018

To the Editor:

Criticizing yesterday's Supreme Court decision "cutting off matching funds to candidates participating in (Arizona's) public campaign finance system," you bemoan the fact that "candidates . . . can no longer receive public funds they had counted on to run against a free-spending wealthy opponent" ("Keeping Politics Safe for the Rich," June 9).

Like candidates for public office, at my blog I often express opinions that I believe would improve the world. Unfortunately, though, I must compete against free-spending wealthy opponents such as you and other giants in the mainstream media. My ideas and I are at a terrible disadvantage. So, using your logic, I conclude that government's failure to give "matching funds" to "qualifying" alternative media—like my blog—is an injustice that keeps Americans poorly informed. The quality of ideas that Americans now carry into voting booths is inferior because government doesn't level the media playing field with such subsidies.

Given the important role of ideas in shaping electoral outcomes, surely you'll not let concerns about freedom of the press prevent you from supporting matching funds for your competitors. Right?

Sincerely,

Donald J. Boudreaux

Underwriters Laboratories, Inc. (UL) sets safety standards for electrical products. Established in 1894, it is a nongovernmental agency that serves North America, Europe, Asia, and Latin America. The electrical industry has no interest in producing unsafe products.

SANCHEZ CLEARLY THOUGHT THAT THIS KID WAS DUMB AS A DUCK.

....

16 March 2009

Mr. Rick Sanchez, Host, CNN NewsRoom
One CNN Center
Atlanta, GA 30303

Dear Mr. Sanchez:

Re your interview today with economics students at Georgia State University: when a young man said that he is skeptical of government regulation and that he values individual liberty, you derisively accused him of believing that the economy would work well "without any rules."

The smug assurance of your accusation reveals your gross misunderstanding of the case for free markets. That case is *not* that rules are unnecessary. Rather, it's that rules written by politicians and enforced by bureaucrats generally work much less well than do rules that emerge decentrally—rules that evolve from the voluntary interactions and successes and mistakes of individuals each pursuing his or her own goals without being herded by a central authority—rules that are enforced by competition and by the exercise of personal responsibility and that, when sufficiently important, become formalized in case law declared by courts.

The distinction between what you think of as rules and the kinds of rules that permeate successful market economies is perhaps subtle. But it's also real and important. You should try to grasp it.

Sincerely,

Donald Boudreaux

FRANCIS SCOTT KEY.

"Hmmm . . . 'land of the free' sounds a bit radical. Maybe we should say 'land of the *fair* and the home of the brave' instead."

TO BE FAIR, THIS GUY LIKELY
KNOWS NO ECONOMICS.

22 November 2010

Editor, The New York Times
620 Eighth Avenue
New York, NY 10018

To the Editor:

Todd Tucker wants Uncle Sam to reject free trade in favor of "fair trade" (Letters, Nov. 22).

While every decent person applauds fairness and condemns unfairness, "fairness" is far too fuzzy a concept to guide public policy. To see why, imagine what the state of First Amendment law would be like were only a few words of that amendment changed to make its guiding principle fairness rather than freedom:

"Congress shall make no unfair law respecting an establishment of religion, or prohibiting the fair exercise thereof; or abridging the fairness of speech, or of the press; or the right of the people fairly to assemble, and to petition the Government fairly for a redress of grievances."

Is there any doubt that replacing "free" with "fair" in this context would remove all teeth from the First Amendment? In the same way, a policy of fair trade rather than free trade would, in practice, be a policy of unfree—and, by the way, unfair—monopoly privileges for politically influential domestic producers.

Sincerely,

Donald J. Boudreaux

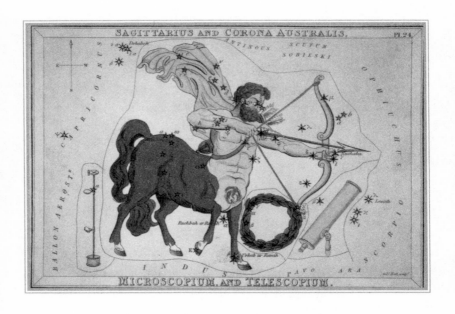

SAGITTARIUS AND CORONA AUSTRALIS, Pl.24

MICROSCOPIUM, AND TELESCOPIUM.

QUESTION: WHAT IS TO ECONOMICS AS ASTROLOGY IS TO ASTRONOMY? (WE BADLY NEED SUCH A TERM.)

....

28 July 2009

Mr. Tom Gjelten, National Public Radio
635 Massachusetts Avenue NW
Washington, DC 20001

Dear Mr. Gjelten:

Reporting yesterday on trade between the U.S. and China, you interviewed University of Maryland economist Peter Morici. Mr. Morici is concerned that trade between these two countries is "imbalanced." His concern is utterly inappropriate.

Trade between the University of Maryland and Mr. Morici is also imbalanced: the University imports more from the Morici household (namely, Mr. Morici's services as a faculty member) than the Morici household imports from the University. Yet I doubt seriously that Mr. Morici would claim that the University is getting a raw deal.

I challenge Mr. Morici to search throughout economic theory for any doctrine that suggests that even the most ideally functioning markets will result in any two economic entities—including any two countries—having "balanced" trade with each other. He'll search in vain.

Sincerely,

Donald J. Boudreaux

★　★　★

"Inheritance taxes are so high
that the happiest mourner at
a rich man's funeral is usually
Uncle Sam."

—Olin Miller

NOTE THE IMPLICIT ASSUMPTIONS IN THE *USA TODAY* EDITOR'S ARGUMENT.

17 December 2010

Editor, USA Today
7950 Jones Branch Drive
McLean, VA 22108-0605

Dear Editor:

Among your chief justifications for the estate tax is that people who inherit wealth didn't earn that wealth and, therefore, don't deserve to get it ("Tax deal showers billions on heirs to the largest estates," Dec. 17).

Overlook the fact that the persons who *did* earn that wealth can choose to bequeath it, or to deny it, to whomever they choose. Instead ask: do the persons who get whatever wealth is collected from the estate tax deserve it?

If the fact that Smith did not personally earn the estate wealth in question is a good reason to keep Smith from inheriting that wealth, what moral justification is there for the likes of Jones and Jackson—who also did not personally earn the wealth in question—to acquire this wealth?

Sincerely,

[signature]

Rear view of Belgian chocolate drink vendor in the 1920s. He might get violent.

HOW ABOUT THAT?!

....

26 March 2009

Editor, The New York Times
620 Eighth Avenue
New York, NY 10018

To the Editor:

While in Mexico, Secretary of State Hillary Clinton will pledge U.S. help in the fight against violent Mexican drug suppliers ("Clinton Says U.S. Feeds Mexico Drug Trade," March 26).

It's interesting to reflect that when Mrs. Clinton visits France she need not pledge U.S. help in the fight against violent French wine suppliers. Or that when she visits Belgium she need not pledge help against violent Belgian chocolate suppliers. Or that when she visits Colombia she need not pledge help against violent Colombian coffee suppliers. Or that when she visits Japan she need not pledge help against violent Japanese automobile suppliers.

I detect a pattern! When goods and services can be produced, sold, and consumed legally, suppliers of these goods and services are peaceful and not violent.

Sincerely,

"Stay local, please. Thank you.
I'm off to my next city."

WELL, NOT THAT LOCAL!

·····································

22 April 2007

Editor, New York Times Book Review
229 West 43rd St.
New York, NY 10036

To the Editor:

That scold of modernity, Bill McKibben, has written a new book advocating the replacement of globalization with local economies—which reviewer Lance Morrow calls "small, localized, communitarian, neighborly" ("Be My Neighbor," April 22).

Surely I'm not the only reader who finds great irony in Mr. Morrow's description of McKibben as "a widely traveled writer."

Sincerely,

[signature]

"I think I'll be keeping my purse, sonny."

ON GUNS AND DETERRENCE.

27 June 2008

Editor, New Orleans Times-Picayune
3800 Howard Avenue
New Orleans, LA 70125-1429

Dear Editor:

The usually thoughtful Eugene Robinson writes that "The practical benefits of effective gun control are obvious: If there are fewer guns, there are fewer shootings and fewer funerals" (June 27). But what's "obvious" at first glance isn't necessarily true.

Much research finds that more guns lead to *less* violent crime. The reason is that would-be violent offenders are less likely to attack persons who might be armed than to attack persons who probably aren't armed. While the relationship between the breadth of gun ownership and crime is an empirical one—this question cannot be answered purely by abstract reasoning—the "more guns, less crime" thesis is not far-fetched. Persons who doubt it should ask themselves if they believe it possible that crime would rise if guns were taken away from police officers. If they answer "yes," then they must concede the real possibility that denying guns to law-abiding private persons also raises the crime rate.

Sincerely,

I gotta see a doctor. It's only 72 degrees outside and I'm sweating like crazy.

MARKET PRICES REFLECT A COMPLEX, UNDERLYING REALITY. THAT REALITY ISN'T CHANGED BY PREVENTING PRICES FROM DOING THEIR JOB.

....

10 May 2008

The Editor, The Economist
25 St James's Street
London SW1A 1HG
United Kingdom

Sir:

Exploring how governments in emerging-market countries might tamp down inflation, you write that one option "is to do nothing apart from slapping on some temporary price controls, and hope that inflation pressures will soon ease" ("Economic focus: A tale of two worlds," May 10).

Trying to control inflation in this way makes no more sense than trying to control the temperature of a room by rigging thermometers so that they never record readings above 72 degrees Fahrenheit.

Sincerely,

Donald Boudreaux

Maybe farm-raised terrapins would be safer than government-protected
terrapins.

ECONOMICS 101.

....

9 February 2007

Editor, The Baltimore Sun
501 N. Calvert Street
Baltimore, Maryland 21278

To the Editor:

You assert that the diamondback terrapin is endangered because "Demand for them as food or pets had skyrocketed" ("Diamondbacks in the rough," Feb. 9). This fact cannot possibly be the full story.

Demand for chicken as food has skyrocketed, yet we hear no talk of chickens being endangered. Likewise, demand for Jack Russell terriers as pets has skyrocketed without casting this breed into the endangered category. The reason is that these animals are privately owned—and their owners have incentives not to slaughter or sell these animals into extinction.

The problem for terrapins is that state ownership of the Chesapeake and other inland waters thwarts private entrepreneurs from establishing private property rights over these animals.

Sincerely,

★ ★ ★

"Ten years ago, the richest person on Earth couldn't buy a device that does what the iPhone does . . . Lifesaving and life-changing medicines and therapies once unknown are now commonplace . . . TV viewers used to have three channels to choose from. Now they have hundreds."

—Steve Chapman, "What Occupy Wall Street is getting totally wrong," *The Chicago Tribune*

MY FATHER—A RETIRED SHIPYARD WORKER—TODAY IS LEARNING TO COOK BY WATCHING THE FOOD NETWORK (WHEN HE'S NOT IN HIS GARAGE FIDDLING AROUND WITH THE LATEST ELECTRIC SCREWDRIVER OR LASER-BEAM LEVEL THAT HE BOUGHT FROM HOME DEPOT FOR LITTLE MORE THAN THE PRICE OF A CUP OF COFFEE).

....

10 February 2008

The Editor, New York Times
620 Eighth Avenue
New York, NY 10018

To the Editor:

Yesterday, columnist Bob Herbert repeated the familiar refrain that America's middle-class is disappearing ("Where's the Big Idea?" February 9). Today, the Dallas Fed's Michael Cox and Richard Alm supply compelling evidence against this tired thesis ("You Are What You Spend," February 10).

As people all across this land, with their cell-phones nearby, watch a gazillion channels on their high-def flat-screen TVs or surf the web wirelessly or use their GPS systems to avoid getting lost while driving to malls in their air-bagged cars and listening to their MP3 players (or, perhaps, to their satellite radios), I do wonder what strange slice of America Mr. Herbert frequents to shield his eyes and ears from today's widespread prosperity.

Sincerely,

Donald J. Boudreaux

ACCORDING TO KRUGMAN, OPPOSITION TO HIGHER TAXES IS THE PRODUCT OF A POLITICAL CULTURE THAT IS "CORRUPT AND DYSFUNCTIONAL."

23 August 2010

Editor, The New York Times
620 Eighth Avenue
New York, NY 10018

To the Editor:

Reasonable people can debate whether or not raising taxes is appropriate, but Paul Krugman isn't reasonable ("Now That's Rich," August 23). Instead, he simplistically insinuates that the proper relationship between Americans and their government is exactly the opposite of what the founders expressly took this relationship to be.

For government not to raise taxes on high-income earners is not for government "to cut checks averaging $3 million each to the richest 120,000 people in the country." No checks will be cut and no money will be taken from anyone.

Income is earned by individuals. It originates as their property and not that of government or of a collective 'us.' Even if this money is deemed necessary to keep Uncle Sam solvent, remember that this government was created to protect individual rights that the founders knew to exist independently of any state. In contrast, according to Mr. Krugman's political dogma, all property originates with government. For him, government is Creator, with each individual a serf living at its pleasure. That belief is the seed of tyranny.

Sincerely,

It all adds up to higher gasoline prices for all of us.

THANKS TO TIBOR MACHAN FOR ALERTING ME TO THIS CROWING.

....

28 January 2008

Editor, New York Times Magazine
620 Eighth Avenue
New York, NY 10018

To the Editor:

Sheryl Crow says about her song "Gasoline" that it "should be perceived as a futuristic song about people who would take to the streets and revolt and take back our freedom from the oppression of gas prices" ("Agit Pop," January 27).

First, some perspective: adjusted for inflation, gasoline at the pump today costs about 20 cents per gallon less than it cost at its peak in March of 1981. Second, just what would people protest? Higher federal taxes at the pump? Perhaps environmental regulations that have transformed a once-national and highly efficient market for refining gasoline into a fragmented hodge-podge struggling to satisfy different state requirements? Or maybe protesters would take aim at government requirements that high-cost ethanol be added to gasoline?

Sincerely,

[signature: Donald J. Boudreaux]

★　★　★

Arnie Celnicker is a former attorney for the FTC and the Antitrust Division of the Justice Department. After leaving the government, he established a consulting business regarding antitrust cases. His private practice benefited from advising on lawsuits such as the one he endorses here.

THE FTC IS TO MARKETS WHAT LARD IS TO HUMAN ARTERIES.

....

7 July 2007

Editor, The Wall Street Journal
200 Liberty Street
New York, NY 10281

To the Editor:

Arnie Celnicker argues that the FTC's challenge of Whole Food's merger with Wild Oats is justified by various "market nuances" (Letters, July 7). Among these is the fact that "financial markets have deprived Wild Oats of the capital to compete head on with Whole Foods" and the fact that consumer demand for organic foods is skyrocketing.

How in the name of free-range chicken do these facts justify government blocking this merger? Precisely because consumers now want more and more organic products, financial markets have every incentive to invest in firms catering to this growing market *if* these firms are well-managed. Wild Oats' inability to get adequate private financing in this growing market is strong evidence that its assets now are poorly managed. It's only natural that Whole Foods spots and seizes this opportunity to use these assets more effectively at meeting consumer demands. The FTC's interference—an unwholesome additive to the market—jeopardizes consumer well-being.

Sincerely,

[signature: Donald J. Boudreaux]

Should our currency rely primarily on trust in God or a sound
monetary policy?

NOT HEAVEN CENT.

2 September 2010

Editor, Washington Post
1150 15th St., NW
Washington, DC 20071

Dear Editor:

Arguing that "In God We Trust" should be displayed more prominently on the dollar coin, Michael Bridges says "The motto is something we should be proud of" (Letters, Sept. 2). Perhaps. But the history of that motto raises serious questions about just what sovereign Americans are being encouraged to trust: God or government?

As Benn Steil and Manuel Hinds point out in their remarkable book *Money, Markets & Sovereignty*, "to create a mystique premium on their coins, whose face value significantly exceeded their intrinsic value, rulers typically adopted religious symbols in their stamps. The less gold, the more God. In fact, 'In God We Trust' was added to American dollar bills only after their gold backing was dropped in 1862."[6]

Sincerely,

[signature]

Quick everyone, it's raining money!

A NEW AND MORE GILDED FANTASY TRAIN
LEAVES THE STATION AT NOON TODAY.

20 January 2009

Editor, The Wall Street Journal
200 Liberty Street
New York, NY 10281

To the Editor:

You report that Barack Obama will call for "a new era of responsibility" ("Obama to Call for a New Era of Responsibility," January 20).

His actions belie his words. By seeking an extra $800 billion for "stimulus," Mr. Obama will generate a typhoon of irresponsibility. Consider what Arnold Kling says at the blog EconLog: "How many people will have meaningful input in determining the overall allocation of the billion stimulus? 10? 20? It won't be more than 1000. These people—let's say that in the end 500 technocrats will play a meaningful role in writing the bill—will have unimaginable power. Remember that what they are doing is taking our money and deciding for us how to spend it. Presumably, that is because they are wiser at spending our money than we are at spending it ourselves.

"The arithmetic is mind-boggling. If 500 people have meaningful input, and the stimulus is almost $800 billion, then on average each person is responsible for taking more than $1.5 billion of our money and trying to spend it more wisely than we would spend it ourselves."[7]

Absolutely no one can spend $1.5 billion of other people's money responsibly.

Sincerely,

Donald J. Boudreaux

Another example of unsafe behavior

AGAIN: THE VALUE OF LIFE ISN'T INFINITE.

....

19 June 2009

Editor, New Orleans Times-Picayune
3800 Howard Avenue
New Orleans, LA 70125-1429

Dear Editor:

Befuddled that many Louisianans don't wish to force motorcyclists to wear helmets, Nicholette Shannon suggests that safety is always more important than what she dismisses as "convenience" (Letters, June 19).

Safety, however, clearly does not always trump convenience. If it did, no one would ever ride a motorcycle to begin with. Indeed, no one would ride in automobiles, jaywalk, or eat fast food. Each of us routinely trades-off some safety to get more convenience. And no one, including Ms. Shannon, should presume that her preferred balance between safety and convenience is or ought to be the preferred balance for other persons.

Sincerely,

Donald Boudreaux

Decade Averages of Weather-Related Deaths

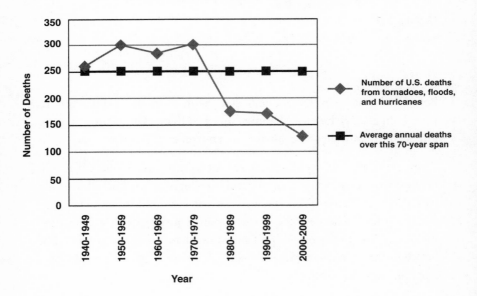

Data are from the U.S. National Weather Service's Office of
Climate, Water and Weather Services:
http://www.nws.noaa.gov/om/hazstats/images/71-years.pdf

BUT I PREDICT A CONTINUING FLOOD OF SUCH PSEUDOSCIENCE FROM THE LIKES OF MCKIBBEN.

24 May 2011

Editor, Washington Post
1150 15th St., NW
Washington, DC 20071

Dear Editor:

Bill McKibben blames recent weather-related deaths on climate change ("A link between climate change and Joplin tornadoes? Never!" May 24). And he snarkily dismisses the argument that humankind can adapt well to such change.

Let's look at data from the National Weather Service on annual fatalities in the U.S. caused by tornados, floods, and hurricanes from 1940 through 2009. The trend is clear and encouraging: the number of such fatalities, especially since 1980, is declining.

The average annual number of such fatalities over this entire 70-year span is 248. From 1940-1979, the average annual number of fatalities was, at 290, higher than 248. But from 1980-2009, the average annual number of fatalities was 194, *lower* than 248.[8]

This decline in the absolute number of deaths caused by tornados, floods, and hurricanes is even more impressive considering that U.S. population more than doubled over these 70 years.

Seems that Mr. McKibben's apocalyptic prognostications about humanity's future are as fact-based as are those of the Rev. Harold Camping.

Sincerely,

William Magear Tweed—widely known as "Boss" Tweed—was an American politician most notable for being the "boss" of Tammany Hall, the Democratic Party political machine that played a major role in the politics of 19th century New York City and State.

Tweed was elected to the United States House of Representatives in 1852, and the New York County Board of Supervisors in 1858, the year he became the "Grand Sachem" of Tammany Hall. Tweed's greatest influence came from being an appointed member of a number of boards and commissions, his control over political patronage in New York City through Tammany, and his ability to ensure the loyalty of voters through jobs he could create and dispense on city-related projects.

Tweed was convicted for stealing an amount estimated by an aldermen's committee in 1877 at between $25 million and $45 million from New York City taxpayers through political corruption, although later estimates ranged as high as $200 million. He died in the Ludlow Street Jail.[9]

THOUGHTLESS PROPOSAL.

· ·

11 January 2010

Editor, Chicago Tribune
435 N. Michigan Avenue
Chicago, IL 60611

Dear Editor:

Seeking to rid politics of the influence of special interests, Jeffrey Smith says that "Our campaigns need 100 percent public financing" (Letters, Jan. 11).

Questions for Mr. Smith: Who would determine which candidates get funding and which do not? Does Mr. Smith not worry that the committee or process chosen for allocating campaign funds will itself be heavily influenced by the very special-interests that now dominate government—and, thus, will only strengthen these interests' strangling grip on the public fisc? Is Mr. Smith blind to the likelihood that giving to government complete control over who runs for office and who doesn't will vastly increase the power of that most dangerous of special-interest groups: incumbent politicians?

Sincerely,

[signature]

Soviet-era joke:

Q: How do you double the value of a lada (Soviet-made car)?

A: Fill it with gas.

OR KLM TO KALAMAZOO!

14 August 2008

Editor, USA Today
7950 Jones Branch Drive
McLean, VA 22108-0605

Dear Editor:

Re: "Nickeled-and-dimed" (August 14):

What would you predict about the quality and price of cars if Uncle Sam allowed *no* foreign auto producers to compete domestically against GM, Ford, and Chrysler? The answer is obvious: Americans would pay exorbitant prices for shoddy cars.

So it's unsurprising that Americans pay exorbitant prices for shoddy air travel: Uncle Sam allows *no* foreign airlines to compete on domestic routes against American-owned carriers.

The quality of air travel would rise and its price fall if Uncle Sam were to allow Americans to choose from among domestic *and* foreign carriers for that flight to Grandma's for Thanksgiving and to the business meeting in Waukesha or Wilmington.

Sincerely,

Courtesy of Boston Public Library

Charles Ponzi made millions of dollars when he promised huge returns on investment but actually paid off early investor with funds from later investors. Social Security, which promises to pay off retirees (early investors) with funds from working people (later investors) is perhaps the biggest Ponzi scheme in history—except for the fact that Charles Ponzi never forced anyone to buy what he was selling.

THIS IS WHAT PASSES FOR INFORMED DISCUSSION.

22 February 2011

Editor, USA Today
7950 Jones Branch Drive
McLean, VA 22108-0605

Dear Editor:

Budget director Jacob Lew assures us that Social Security is solvent because the Social Security "trust fund" contains lots of U.S. Treasury bonds "backed with the full faith and credit of the U.S. government— and are held in reserve for when revenue collected is not enough to pay the benefits due" ("Social Security isn't the problem," Feb. 22).

Yes, the Social Security "trust fund" is indeed filled with ample quantities of interest-bearing U.S. treasuries. But the same organization (Uncle Sam) that is the creditor on these treasuries is also the debtor on them. Ask: when Uncle Sam cashes in these treasuries to get funds to pay promised Social Security benefits, who pays Uncle Sam the principal and interest on these treasuries? Answer: Uncle Sam—who must, of course, raise taxes on flesh-and-blood people to get the dollars that he pays to himself so that he can then pay out promised Social Security benefits.

I.O.U.s written to one's self are not assets. They are, instead, pathetic reminders of one's gross financial irresponsibility.

Bernie Madoff is in jail—rightly so—for duping people with the same sort of financial flim-flammery that the White House budget director today peddles in your pages.

Sincerely,

This ghost town 'cured' its problem of population growth.

ANOTHER ANGLE.
....

27 November 2010

Editor, The Wall Street Journal
1211 6th Ave.
New York, NY 10036

To the Editor:

Bill Gates writes that "slowing population growth" has "proven . . . to be critical to long-term economic growth" ("Africa Needs Aid, Not Flawed Theories," Nov. 27). What's the evidence for this claim?

Did Hong Kong grow as a result of slowing population growth? No. What about Taiwan over the past 60 years? No. Was slowing population growth key to England's unprecedented economic blossoming during the industrial revolution? No. Did population growth in America slow before its economy began to grow? No.

Did the great 20th century migration to California cause that state's economy to languish? No. Do the high population densities of Manhattan, London, Sydney, and Singapore keep people in those cities poor? No. Do low population densities in the Republic of Congo, Chad, and Bolivia make people in those countries rich? No.

It's disappointing that Mr. Gates, visionary entrepreneur that he is, so readily accepts the pop myth that population growth is a drag on economic growth.

Sincerely,

[signature: Donald J. Boudreaux]

⭐ ⭐ ⭐

"Our research shows that blacks comprise 62.7 percent and whites 36.7 percent of all drug offenders admitted to state prison, even though federal surveys and other data detailed in this report show clearly that this racial disparity bears scant relation to racial differences in drug offending. There are, for example, five times more white drug users than black. Relative to population, black men are admitted to state prison on drug charges at a rate that is 13.4 times greater than that of white men. In large part because of the extraordinary racial disparities in incarceration for drug offenses, blacks are incarcerated for all offenses at 8.2 times the rate of whites. One in every 20 black men over the age of 18 in the United States is in state or federal prison, compared to one in 180 white men."

—Human Rights Watch, "Racial Disparities in the War on Drugs"[10]

COLLATERAL DAMAGE.
....

24 February 2011

Editor, USA Today
7950 Jones Branch Drive
McLean, VA 22108-0605

Dear Editor:

Thurgood Marshall indeed deserves high praise for his work to rid the United States of Jim Crow legislation ("Thurgood Marshall blazed a path for civil rights," Feb. 18). But while on the U.S. Supreme Court, he turned a blind eye to an institution that disproportionately imprisons, disenfranchises, and discriminates against blacks: the war on drugs.

Interviewed in 1987 by *Life*, Justice Marshall said "If it's a dope case, I won't even read the petition. I ain't giving no break to no dope dealer."[11]

Quite apart from the question of whether or not drugs should be legalized, Justice Marshall's practice of automatically siding with the government in every drug case gave a free pass to government officials not only to violate the Constitution in their pursuit of alleged drug offenders, but also to act on whatever bigotry and prejudices they might have had as long as these officials could claim that their actions were part of the drug war.

Sincerely,

Donald Boudreaux

If a corporation treads on consumers, it goes broke. If government treads on consumers, we go broke.

FETISH FOR FORCE.

20 February 2010

Editor, The New York Times
620 Eighth Avenue
New York, NY 10018

To the Editor:

In his dismissal of the Tea Partiers, Keith Ensminger—who embraces "Progressivism"—says that "They want government off their back, which means corporations are free to act in any way" (Letters, Feb. 20).

Mr. Ensminger's understanding hasn't progressed beyond 1930s-era New Dealism. Competition and consumer choice, not government, are the chief means of ensuring that corporations act in the public interest. The "Progressivism" that he asserts is necessary to constrain corporations does quite the opposite. That naïve mindset has given us corporate bailouts, subsidies for corporate exports, tariffs that excuse corporations from having to compete with foreign rivals, and bureaucratic agencies that, pretending to work for the general welfare, more often than not are captured by the very corporations that they are ostensibly meant to regulate.

If a corporation, without government protection, offers Mr. Ensminger a product he doesn't like, he can simply refuse to buy it. Government, though, doesn't offer; it commands. If he doesn't like what he is commanded to do, he has no choice but to obey. What's so "progressive" about that?

Sincerely,

Used with permission of the Simon Family.

THE BET

Julian Simon was a professor of Business Administration who published many books and articles on economic subjects. He challenged the theory of Paul Ehrlich that population growth inevitably leads to resource shortages.

In 1980 Simon offered Ehrlich the chance to pick any five metals he wished. Simon bet him $1,000 that the inflation-adjusted price of the bundle of the five metals would be lower in ten years, indicating plenty, not shortage. Ehrlich chose tin, nickel, tungsten, chromium, and copper. Ten years later, the price of each of the five metals had fallen, just as Simon predicted. Ehrlich lost the bet. Simon argued that the ultimate resource is not a commodity, but human ingenuity—and that greater population leads to more discoveries and solutions and, hence, greater access to natural resources.

SOME OF THESE PEOPLE LONG TO BE "LOCAVORES"—EATING ONLY LOCALLY GROWN FOODS. THE LAST TIME MOST PEOPLE WERE LOCAVORES MOST PEOPLE WERE MALNOURISHED.

16 February 2008

The Editor, New York Times
620 Eighth Avenue
New York, NY 10018

To the Editor:

How distressing that many Americans now worry themselves sick that their consumption habits are ruining the environment ("Well, Doctor, I Have This Recycling Problem," February 16). There is, however, no need for them to seek professional help. My three-step plan to cure this mental anguish is simple and guaranteed to work:

Step One: Avoid major newspapers, magazines, and network news. These media uncritically genuflect to the official creed of environmental groups and never give any historical perspective.

Step Two: Get historical perspective by learning how filthy and perilous the environment was before modern capitalism. I recommend reading Fernand Braudel's *The Structures of Everyday Life*.

Step Three: Get the actual facts about today's state of humanity and the environment by reading the data-packed works of Indur Goklany, Bjorn Lomborg, and Julian Simon.

Persons completing this regimen will feel supreme contentment whenever they buy things such as SUVs, non-fair-trade, non-organic coffee from Guatemala, and even incandescent light bulbs.

Sincerely,

How dare you take money earned in America and spend it outside our country!

HORRORS!
....

14 August 2010

Editor, Washington Times
3600 New York Ave NE
Washington, DC 20002

Dear Editor:

Haydee Pavia writes that "The majority of [Mexican] illegal aliens come here to attain the American dream and take it back to their native country. These scofflaws don't come here because of idealism, but for the wealth they can acquire and one day take back to their native country" (Letters, August 14).

Suppose that Ms. Pavia's claim is correct. So what? The vast majority of these immigrants acquire their wealth by working—a fact that means that the wealth that immigrants accumulate while in America is paid to them voluntarily.

That is, these immigrants acquire wealth only by creating goods and services that are valued by the Americans who hire or otherwise do business with them. The process that Ms. Pavia describes and dislikes benefits both working immigrants and Americans, regardless of whether or not immigrants take their earnings back to Mexico.

We should encourage such immigration rather than dismiss it on the grounds that the typical immigrant might be motivated by ideals no more lofty than those that prompt the typical American to rise from bed each morning in order to earn a living.

Sincerely,

[signature]

CLOWNS.
··············

2 August 2009

Editor, Los Angeles Times
202 West 1st Street
Los Angeles, California 90012

Dear Editor:

You report that Uncle Sam is on the verge of paying the City of Los Angeles $30 million to subsidize a ten-year run of Cirque du Soleil ("L.A. City Council considers $30 million loan for Cirque du Soleil," August 2).

So it's finally come to pass—America has embarked on the same road down which ancient Rome marched to its ruin: Uncle Sam not only subsidizes bread (by subsidizing wheat production) but now also circuses.

Sincerely,

FREEDOM DOES INDEED HAVE ITS PRICE.

26 May 2009

Editor, New York Post
1211 Avenue of the Americas
New York, NY 10036-8790

Dear Editor:

Ralph Peters argues that terror suspects should be executed summarily, as "man-killing animals" possessing no rights ("Instant Justice," May 26).

His argument begs the question of whether or not those suspected of being terrorists really *are* terrorists. Like too many on the political right (and some on the left), Mr. Peters assumes that procedural protections for persons accused of wrongdoing exist primarily to make life easier for the accused. Not so. The chief functions of these protections are two. One is to shield innocent persons from being wrongly convicted and punished. The other is to keep the state's powers in check.

A state that can summarily execute anyone whom it assures its citizens is a dangerous terrorist will itself, in time, become the most dangerous of terrorists.

Sincerely,

J osef Stalin ruled the Soviet Union from 1929 to 1953. His tenure
can be defined by three primary policies:

1. FIVE YEAR PLANS: He instituted five year plans run by the
   government to improve economic output. Despite the ability
   to harshly punish workers with fines, withheld pay, and even
   prison, not one of the five-year goals set during his leadership
   was ever achieved.

2. COLLECTIVIZATION: The government seized all small
   farms given to the Russian peasantry by Lenin and collectivized
   them to improve agricultural production. Production of grain,
   cattle, pigs, sheep, and goats all declined precipitously from
   1928 to 1934 after implementation of the government plan.

3. PURGES: Stalin is famous for having said, "Death solves all
   problems. No person, no problem."

THERE ARE EXCEPTIONS, OF COURSE, BUT THE TYPICAL BUSINESS EXECUTIVE'S UNDERSTANDING OF ECONOMICS IS PATHETICALLY WEAK.

2 September 2008

Editor, The Wall Street Journal
200 Liberty Street
New York, NY 10281

To the Editor:

Crusading for a national "energy plan" and upset that Holman Jenkins isn't on board, T. Boone Pickens asks rhetorically: "My father used to tell me that a fool with a plan is better than a genius with no plan. So I ask, what's Mr. Jenkins's plan?" (Letters, Sept. 2).

Contrary to Mr. Pickens's assumption, an economy is not simply a gigantic business firm. An economy is both incomprehensibly more complex than is even the largest multinational corporation, and it has no specific, overriding purpose comparable to a firm's goal of maximizing profits—a purpose by which the performance of each employee and each investment decision is relatively easy to evaluate. So while plans and some measure of central direction make sense for firms, comparable plans and direction for an economy are poison. They prevent the on-going decentralized experimentation from which spring not only progress that is unplanned, but progress whose details could not have been foreseen before they actually materialize.

The Soviet Union famously had plans for its economy; the United States did not. Which country was the fool?

Sincerely,

37.52 17.12 1.81%
17.02 42.15 +0.75 0.48%
40.86 27.09 +0.13 2.09%
26.07 22.47 +0.46 -5.12%
21.71 23.37 -1.26 3.30%
22.74 +12.51
377.43 0.78%
93.96 95.61 +0.74 1.69%
24.74 25.22 +0.42 1.22%
24.35 24.82 +0.30
55.00

HENRY MANNE IS CORRECT TO CALL PROHIBITIONS ON INSIDER TRADING "COCKAMAMIE."

19 October 2009

Editor, The New York Times
620 Eighth Avenue
New York, NY 10018

To the Editor:

Did Raj Rajaratnam really trade on inside information ("Arrest of Hedge Fund Chief Unsettles the Industry," Oct. 19)? I don't know. But let's assume that the government's charges against him are accurate.

The more germane question is: should insider trading be illegal? The great corporate-law scholar Henry Manne made a strong case, in his 1966 book *Insider Trading and the Stock Market*, that insider trading is the opposite of harmful; it's beneficial.

Markets work more efficiently the more rapidly and fully prices adjust to reflect the true value of goods, services, and assets. Trades made on inside information are an important source of such price adjustments. Insider trading—by causing prices to adjust to insiders' information—speeds up the wholesome process of making inside information public.

Just imagine, for example, how much wealth would have been preserved and how many dreams left unshattered had Enron insiders—who knew of the fraudulent practices of Ken Lay, Jeff Skilling, and other top Enron executives—felt free ten years ago to trade on their inside information. Enron's share prices would have fallen much earlier, and those executives' fraudulent practices been exposed much sooner, were insider trading not illegal.

Sincerely,

Donald J. Boudreaux

Americans being forced to buy products through advertising

COMMERCIAL HAL.

. . . .

7 April 2010

Editor, Washington Post
1150 15th St., NW
Washington, DC 20071

Dear Editor:

Harold Meyerson is appalled that producers of branded consumer products help to fund—and, hence, get their products featured in—many
Hollywood movies ("Moviemaking becomes commercial art," April 7).

Is he equally appalled that the very same Internet pages on which his
column appears today are funded in part by—and, hence, feature ads
for—Open Skies Airlines, Ryan Homes, Sprint, Fidelity Investments,
and (egads!) the American Petroleum Institute? Should your readers
conclude that the quality and sincerity of the Post's news reports and
opinion pieces are compromised by appearing on the same computer
screen as ads for a wide array of commercial products? And will Mr.
Meyerson have the moral mettle to refuse from now on to write for the
Post as long as you continue your cheap and compromising practice of
accepting ads from philistine capitalists?

Sincerely,

[signature]

Ritz-Carlton, New York

GIVING VS. GIVING BACK.

27 April 2011

The Ritz-Carlton Hotel Company
4445 Willard Avenue, Suite 800
Chevy Chase, Maryland 20815

Dear Ritz-Carlton:

Thanks for your e-mail celebrating your "Give Back Getaways"—activities in which you "give back to the community."

Have you taken something that isn't yours? If so, give it back! (But don't applaud yourself for doing so.) If, though, you've not taken anything that doesn't belong to you, you possess nothing that you can give *back*.

Being a profitable corporation, you certainly possess something that you can *give*; and I applaud the generosity that prompts you to do so. But unless your profits come from your wrongdoing, please drop the rhetoric of "giving *back*." Such talk implies that you have something that isn't rightfully yours. It fuels the myth that corporate profits are ill-gotten gains.

Because almost all market exchanges are positive-sum deals, your business success means that you create wealth. You value the $$ you get for renting a hotel room more than you value keeping that room vacant, and your guests value the opportunity to rent that room more than they value whatever else they might have bought with the $$ they pay to you. You gain. Your guests gain. No one loses. Wealth is created.

By all means, *give* if your shareholders approve. But stop calling it "giving *back*." Your profits aren't pirate booty; they're legitimate earnings.

Sincerely,

Donald J Boudreaux

Thanks to the Equal Care Act, none of you really need medical care right now, don't worry!

REALITY AIN'T OPTIONAL.

....

10 January 2011

Editor, USA Today
7950 Jones Branch Drive
McLean, VA 22108-0605

Dear Editor:

While the term "death panel" is over-the-top, the concern that sparks the use of this term is real and justified ("Nonsense about 'death panels' springs back to life," Jan. 10).

As you recognize, resources for supplying medical care are scarce, and will remain so forever. This fact means that much medical care that would be provided in a world without scarcity must go unprovided in reality. And so the question arises: who decides which medical treatments to undergo and which to forego?

To the extent that government is charged with supplying medical care—either directly or by paying for it—the entity that will unavoidably answer the above question is government. Decisions about which treatments to pursue and for how long will, of necessity, be removed from patients and their families. These decisions will instead be made by strangers.

Call this impersonal decision-making process what you will. Government cannot be given greater responsibility for supplying health care without also being given greater power to deny life-saving treatments—and the duty, in many cases, to do so.

Sincerely,

Donald J. Boudreaux

Washington's Idea of Austerity

One Percent Budgetary Cut in Spending

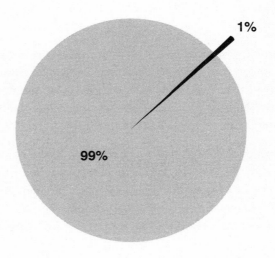

OR AS ARNOLD KLING OF HTTP://ECONLOG.ECONLIB.ORG/ PUTS IT, "SOMEHOW, WE COULD RATCHET UP SPENDING BY HUNDREDS OF BILLIONS AT THE DROP OF A HAT. REDUCING SPENDING BY LESS THAN $100 BILLION BECOMES ARMAGEDDON."

....

9 April 2011

Editor, Washington Post
1150 15th St., NW
Washington, DC 20071

Dear Editor:

Suppose that in a mere three years your family's spending—*spending*, mind you, not income—jumped from $80,000 to $101,600. You're now understandably worried about the debt you're piling up as a result of this 27 percent rise in spending.

So mom and dad, with much drama and angst and finger-pointing about each other's irresponsibility and insensitivity, stage marathon sessions of dinner-table talks to solve the problem. They finally agree to reduce the family's annual spending from $101,600 to $100,584.

For this 1 percent cut in their spending, mom and dad congratulate each other. And to emphasize that this spending cut shows that they are responsible stewards of the family's assets, they approvingly quote Sen. Harry Reid, who was party to similar negotiations that concluded last night on Capitol Hill—negotiations in which Congress agreed to cut 1 percent from a budget that rose 27 percent in just three years. Said Sen. Reid: "Both sides have had to make tough choices. But tough choices is what this job's all about" ("Government shutdown averted: Congress agrees to budget deal, stopgap funding," April 9).

What a joke.

Sincerely,

Donald Boudreaux

A Great Deregulator

THE WORST U.S. PRESIDENT OF MY LIFETIME IS EITHER LBJ OR BUSH II (WITH NIXON COMING IN A CLOSE THIRD).

....

23 May 2007

Editor, New York Post
1211 Avenue of the Americas
New York, NY 10036-8790

To the Editor:

I'm no fan of Jimmy Carter, but conservatives now lathered-up by the former President's criticisms of the current President need a reality check (Letters, May 23).

These conservatives forget that Carter's presidency launched the deregulation of airlines, trucking, and railroads, and that Mr. Carter appointed inflation hawk Paul Volcker as Fed Chairman.

They forget also that Bush II created an obnoxious prescription-drug entitlement program; that he expanded federal control over education; that he shamelessly raised tariffs for blatant political gain; and that he increased discretionary spending faster than did LBJ. And while many conservatives applaud the war in Iraq, not all do. George Will, for example, correctly recognizes that civil society abroad can no more be built by U.S. armed forces than civil society at home can be built by U.S. bureaucrats.

Sincerely,

Donald J. Boudreaux

0018. Hyde Park. Queens Birthday. London.

"By the 1890s . . . most middle-class British families devoted 10 percent of their income for charitable works—an outlay from average family income second only to expenditures on food. Total voluntary giving in Britain was greater than the entire budgets of several European governments, and more than half a million women worked as full-time volunteers for various charitable organizations."

—Richard M. Ebeling, "Book Review,"
Freedom Daily[12]

GOVERNMENT AIN'T US.

....

30 May 2008
Editor, Washington Post
1150 15th St., NW
Washington, DC 20071

Dear Editor:

Michael Gerson asserts that conservative and libertarian advocates of
limited government would "invite genuine statism" by "leaving great
social needs unmet" ("The Libertarian Jesus," May 30). Not so.

We advocates of strictly limited government emphatically do not propose to leave social needs unmet but, instead, to deal with these needs
through non-governmental means. Now perhaps we're mistaken; perhaps non-governmental means will be inferior to government action.
But for Mr. Gerson simply to assume that those of us seeking to scale
back government necessarily want to leave "great social needs unmet"
reveals intellectual laziness on his part—a thoughtless equating of "government" with "society," and an obliviousness to history and a rich intellectual tradition explaining how people operating privately can, and do,
supply a wide range of public goods.

Sincerely,

Used with permission of The Associated Press,
Copyright © 2011. All right reserved.

DOG BITES MAN.

· ·

23 January 2009

Editor, Washington Times
3600 New York Ave NE
Washington, DC 20002

Dear Editor:

Re your headline "Top bailout recipients also major lobbyists" (Jan. 23): While I appreciate the appropriateness of this headline, it's discouraging to realize that such a fact is newsworthy.

If people were as credulous about non-politicians as they are about politicians, we'd routinely read headlines such as "Thief Steals Money to Benefit Himself!" or "Teenage Boys Buy 'Playboy' for the Pictures, Not the Articles" or "18-year-old Italian Supermodel Marries 98-year-old Billionaire Only for His Money!"

Sincerely,

[signature: Donald J. Boudreaux]

Is this child happy or unhappy? Only a government-funded researcher can give us the right answer.

UNHAPPY RESEARCH.

·····································

14 March 2011

Editor, The New York Times
620 Eighth Avenue
New York, NY 10018

To the Editor:

Roger Cohen is impressed with modern-day "happiness" researchers who conclude that economic prosperity does little to make people happier ("The Happynomics of Life," March 13).

Mr. Cohen and these researchers should read Deirdre McCloskey's *Bourgeois Dignity*. She writes the following about the methods used by 'happiness' researchers who employ "self-reported declarations" about how each surveyed person ranks his or her happiness on a scale of, say, one to three, with "two" being "pretty happy" and "three" being "very happy": "An interviewer surprises you on the street, puts a microphone in your face, and demands to know 'Which is it, 1, 2, or 3?' Even the technical problems with such calculations are formidable. For one thing, a noninterval scale is being treated as an interval scale, as though a unit of 1.0 between 2 and 3 were God's own view of the differences between 'pretty' and 'very.' It would be like measuring temperature by asking people to rate things as 'pretty hot' = 2, 'very hot' = 3, and expecting to build a science of thermodynamics on the 'measurements' thus generated."[13]

This research is an unhappy means for achieving deeper understanding.

Sincerely,

Donald J. Boudreaux

What is the ultimate goal of baking a pie? To consume it.

PROTECTIONISTS MAKE TARGETS
THAT ARE ALMOST TOO EASY.

29 September 2009

Editor, The Washington Times
3600 New York Ave NE
Washington, DC 20002

Dear Editor:

Protectionist William Hawkins accuses Adam Smith of being "dreadfully wrong" to insist that the ultimate goal of economic activity is consumption rather than production (Letters, Sept. 27).

Alas, the dreadfully wrong one is Mr. Hawkins. He confuses means with ends. Flour, sugar, apples, an oven, and labor are necessary ingredients for baking an apple pie, but these means are valuable in this use only if someone wants to consume the pie. If no one wants to eat apple pie, then using these ingredients to produce the pie would be wasteful.

Adam Smith correctly understood that the desire to consume is what justifies production, and not vice-versa. If Mr. Hawkins were correct that the ultimate goal of economic activity is production, then he should be just as pleased to have a fresh-from-the-oven sawdust-and-earthworm pie for dessert as he is to have an apple pie.

Sincerely,

Donald J. Boudreaux

The entire population of the world can fit within the city limits of
Jacksonville, with 3.5 square feet per person.

THIS PERSON CALLS ME AN "APOSTATE FROM THE RANKS OF US WHO CARE ABOUT THE EARTH."

5 March 2011

Mr./Ms. "Bill McKibben"

Dear Mr./Ms. "McKibben":

You ask me by e-mail how I can "be so lame and uninformed" not to "realize" that the earth is "overcrowded; overused; over its limit of sustaining life." I ask you: where's the evidence that humanity is on the verge of calamity? Show me hard evidence of general resource depletion. Show me hard evidence that the quality of human life is falling, or destined to fall, over time. Show me hard evidence of overcrowding.

There's plenty of evidence against your propositions; show me some evidence to support them.

Actually, it's coincidental that you mention overcrowding. Just this morning my friend Barry Connor sent me the following e-mail: "If all (7 billion) people on earth were given an area of 3.5 sq. ft. (18" x 28"), they all could stand in the City of Jacksonville, Florida. This calculation is accurate. Check it out. Literally, we have barely scratched the surface of the earth."

True, 3.5 square feet per person ain't much room, but Jacksonville is only a tiny fraction of all land in the U.S.; its size is a rounding error in relation to the amount of land in the earth's temperate zones.

Do you have contrary evidence or arguments that the earth is, in fact, overcrowded?

Sincerely,

211471 FALL INTERNS-

Senator Sherrod Brown seeks highly motivated students for full-and part-time Unpaid Internships for the fall semester (minimum 15 per week). College students and recent graduates are welcome to apply, but preference is given to applicants with Massachusetts ties. Press, scheduling, and legistlative intern opportunities are available. For additional information, please visit http://scottbrown.senate.gov/public/index.cfm/internprogram. Applicants should fax resume and cover letter expressing areas of interest to 202-228-2646.

Who wants to be an unpaid intern for the man fighting to raise the minimum wage?

THANKS TO JIM SWIFT FOR ALERTING ME TO SEN. SHERROD BROWN'S EFFORT TO EXPLOIT HELPLESS EMPLOYEES. (BTW, SEN. BROWN SO FAR REFUSES TO DEBATE FREE TRADE WITH ME.)

4 October 2010

Sen. Sherrod Brown (D-Ohio)
Capitol Hill
Washington, DC

Dear Sen. Brown:

Your office is advertising for an unpaid intern—one whose responsibilities will be quite extensive.[14]

But on your webpage you boast of your efforts to fight poverty by raising the national minimum-wage.[15]

Are you not concerned that you are promoting poverty by paying this intern an hourly wage of $0.00? Or are young men and women who choose to build their resume by working free of charge for you more intelligent and far-sighted than are young men and women who would—were it not illegal to do so—choose to build their resumes by working in the private sector at wages below the legislated minimum? If not—that is, if your interns aren't generally more smart and prudent than are young people who seek employment in the private sector—then why do you continue to deny non-government employees the right to choose the terms of their own employment?

Sincerely,

Who creates more wealth: a foreign wastrel or a responsible investor?

R. ROBERTS VS. P. KRUGMAN.

12 March 2007

Editor, The Wall Street Journal
200 Liberty Street
New York, NY 10281

To the Editor:

Kudos to my colleague Russ Roberts for reminding us that fears today of China's investments in dollar-denominated assets are as foolish as were fears 20 years ago of Japan's investments in these assets ("Protectionists Never Learn," March 12). I hope Paul Krugman reads Russ's essay.

In his June 27, 2005, *New York Times* column, Krugman argued that China does pose a problem today for the U.S. because the Chinese differ from the Japanese: "One difference is that, judging from early indications, the Chinese won't squander their money as badly as the Japanese did."

What a peculiar theory Krugman peddles: we Americans should welcome foreign investors only if they are wastrels. Responsible investors, Krugman believes, are a threat.

Krugman's theory sounds to me a lot like pop internationalism.

Sincerely,

Donald Boudreaux

$2.50

$15,000

NO PARADOX.

· · · · · · · · · · · · · · · · · ·

14 September 2009

Ms. Bridget Quigg
PayScale.com

In "10 Surprising Minimum-Wage Jobs," appearing today at Yahoo News, you wonder why many jobs that are crucial to our well-being, such as emergency medical technician, pay so little.

Economists pose a similar question—namely, why does water (which is utterly essential to life) fetch such a low price while diamonds (utterly inessential) fetch a high price? The answer is that the supply of water relative to its demand is unusually high, so acquiring one additional gallon of water is far easier—that is, far less costly—than acquiring one additional diamond. And for this fact we should be grateful, for it means that the supplies of especially important things such as water and EMT services are wonderfully abundant.

If the market wages of the likes of emergency medical technicians and of preschool teachers were unusually *high*, that would be unfortunate, as high wages in those fields would reflect a lower supply of—and, thus, more-limited use of—these important services.

Sincerely,

Donald Boudreaux

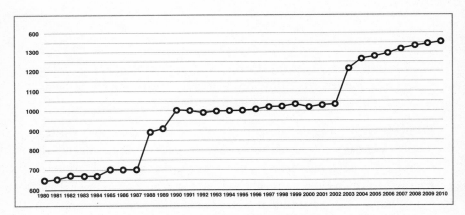

Global Proved Reserves of Petroleum

Data are from the iae.org:
http://www.iae.org.ar/archivos/reservas5.pdf

SLICK ARGUMENT.

·······················

15 March 2011

Editor, USA Today
7950 Jones Branch Drive
McLean, VA 22108-0605

Dear Editor:

Roland Hwang argues that "America consumes roughly one-quarter of
the world's oil, yet we are home to less than 2% of the globe's proven
oil reserves. So much for 'drill, baby, drill.' Even if we were to drill a
hole everywhere in the country that has oil and drain every drop, we'd
have enough to last us just about three years" ("Mideast crisis fuels new
debate on oil," March 15).

Whatever good arguments there might be for not easing restrictions on
drilling, Mr. Hwang's isn't among them. The reason is that the size of
any nation's proved oil reserves is in part an artifact of that nation's policies on drilling. Here's how the Society of Petroleum Engineers defines
"proved reserves":

"Proved reserves are those quantities of petroleum which, by analysis
of geological and engineering data, can be estimated with reasonable
certainty to be commercially recoverable, from a given date forward,
from known reservoirs and under current economic conditions, operating methods, and government regulations."[16]

So the very fact that Uncle Sam prohibits drilling on, say, ANWR keeps
America's proved reserves lower than they would be without this prohi-
bition. The current small size of proved petroleum reserves, therefore,
cannot legitimately be cited as a reason not to ease drilling restrictions.

Sincerely,

Donald J Boudreaux

The path to full employment

A RICKSHAW ECONOMY.
....

24 February 2009

Editor, Boston Globe
P.O. Box 55819
Boston, MA 02205-5819

Dear Editor:

Derrick Z. Jackson reasons that among mass transit's benefits is the fact that, dollar for dollar, its provision requires more workers than do investments in the auto, oil, coal, and gas industries ("The transformation of transportation," Feb. 24). Mr. Jackson's reasoning is flawed.

The number of workers required to supply a good or service is not a benefit of that good or service; it's a cost. Societies become more prosperous only as they succeed in using fewer workers and other inputs to supply any given amount of output. Only then are inputs made available to produce outputs that otherwise could not be produced.

If Mr. Jackson were correct that a project's benefits rise with the number of jobs it creates, then an even better system of public transportation would be rickshaws, for they require one worker for every passenger-ride.

Sincerely,

[signature]

Enemy of the People?

MORE ON AN INSIDIOUS ALLEGATION.

6 November 2006

Editor, The Baltimore Sun
501 N. Calvert Street
Baltimore, Maryland 21278

Dear Editor:

Your lead editorial today correctly notes that China's "booming economy" has lifted 43 million people in that country out of hunger ("On the table," Nov. 6). This boom, of course, is driven by China's move toward free markets and its integration into the global economy.

But also in today's edition, Cynthia Tucker calls globalization "a force more insidious" than terrorism ("Lack of economic security is no less a threat than terrorism," Nov. 6). Does she really believe what she writes? Does she really believe that peaceful commerce with persons in other countries is more insidious than murdering and maiming innocent people? Does she really believe that foreigners who offer to sell televisions and textiles to us are more insidious than those who take our lives and destroy our property?

Sincerely,

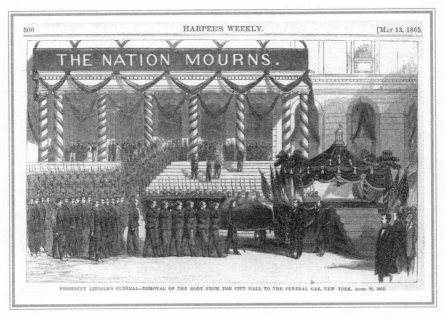

THE NATION MOURNS.

PRESIDENT LINCOLN'S FUNERAL—REMOVAL OF THE BODY FROM THE CITY HALL TO THE FUNERAL CAR, NEW YORK, APRIL 25, 1865.

President Lincoln's funeral—removal of the body from the City Hall to the funeral car, New York

BURY MONOPOLISTS.

••••••••••••••••••••••••••••••

13 August 2010

Editor, USA Today
7950 Jones Branch Drive
McLean, VA 22108-0605

Dear Editor:

Kudos to Scott Bullock, Jeff Rowes, and their colleagues at the Institute for Justice for defending the right of monks at St. Joseph Abbey in Louisiana to sell caskets—and, hence, for defending the right of people to buy caskets from whomever they please ("In defense of monks and free enterprise," August 13).

I have personal evidence that Louisiana's requirement that all caskets be bought from a licensed funeral director is simply meant to protect funeral directors from competition.

When my mother died in 2008, a friend recommended that we bury her in a casket from St. Joseph Abbey. While making arrangements at the funeral home—but before we mentioned an Abbey casket to the funeral director—my family and I were shown several caskets that the home offered for sale. All were pricey. When we finally mentioned that we were considering a casket from St. Joseph Abbey, the funeral director suddenly remembered that he offered some less-expensive caskets. Only then did he show us his more competitively priced models.

Sincerely,

Who do we want to help: The poorest workers or the unionized workers?

WELL-MEANING?
....

16 January 2009

Editor, The New York Times
620 Eighth Avenue
New York, NY 10018

To the Editor:

In his otherwise excellent column "Where Sweatshops Are a Dream" (January 15), Nicholas Kristof writes that "Mr. Obama and the Democrats who favor labor standards in trade agreements mean well, for they intend to fight back at oppressive sweatshops abroad."

Unlikely. Mr. Obama and the Democrats (and Republicans, too) are far less interested in helping poor foreigners than they are in winning votes from American workers and factory owners who compete with producers in poor countries. Given that Mr. Kristof is correct that sweatshops provide a way out of poverty for many of the world's poorest people—and given also that even the lowest-income American worker enjoys a standard of living that is princely compared to that of the typical third-world worker—efforts by western politicians to "save" foreign workers from sweatshops should be labeled properly: heartless and greedy attempts by rich western politicians to win votes from rich western citizens at the expense of the world's poorest workers.

Sincerely,

Donald J. Boudreaux

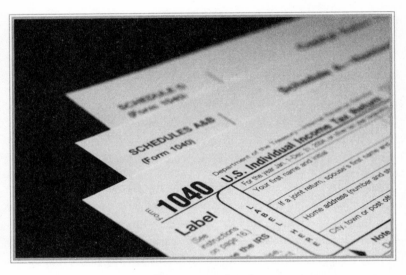

Payment optional

OF COURSE, IN THE CASE OF TAX PENALTIES, THE AGENCY IS UNACCOUNTABLE AND THE CHARGES ARE UNCONSCIONABLE—YET THEY STILL DO ENCOURAGE FULL AND TIMELY PAYMENT OF TAXES.

....

24 August 2010

Editor, The Wall Street Journal
1211 6th Ave.
New York, NY 10036

To the Editor:

You're correct that the Credit Card Accountability, Responsibility and Disclosure Act of 2009 will discourage lenders from extending credit to households most in need of it by arbitrarily reducing the penalties that lenders may assess against dead-beat and delinquent debtors ("The Politics of Plastic," August 24). Our Leaders, though, cling to their peculiar faith that regulations never create incentives for people to do what Our Leaders would prefer people not to do.

Let's put this faith to a real test: Ask Congress and the White House to regulate more strictly the penalties assessed by the IRS against dead-beat and delinquent taxpayers—for example, let's reduce fees and interest charges for late payment of taxes, and eliminate jail time as a punishment for tax evasion. If Our Leaders' faith is sound, there will be no increase in tax evasion and delinquencies. Revenue collected by the IRS will be unaffected. The IRS's stiff penalties will be seen to have been unjustified because (if Our Leaders' faith is true) these penalties do nothing to encourage timely and full payment of taxes.

Sincerely,

Donald Boudreaux

John D. Rockefeller: Environmentally sensitive before his time?

YET ANOTHER EXAMPLE OF A MEMBER OF THE PROFESSORIATE WHOSE IGNORANCE OF HISTORY IS UNPARDONABLE OR WHOSE DISTORTED ETHICS ARE APPALLING (OR BOTH).

....

1 March 2011

Editor, The New York Times
620 Eighth Avenue
New York, NY 10018

To the Editor:

Regardless of the ethics of the L.S.E. accepting money from the Qaddafi Foundation, it is obscene for Professor Meghnad Desai to try to justify the L.S.E.'s actions by saying that "Academic research needs money—Rockefeller was a robber baron once, but we take his money" ("London School of Economics Wrestles With Qaddafi Donation," March 1).

John D. Rockefeller earned every cent of his wealth honestly and peacefully—mostly by creating unprecedented efficiencies in the production and distribution of kerosene, the chief product extracted from petroleum during the 19th century. Rockefeller's efficiencies drove the price of kerosene down from 26 cents per gallon in 1870 (the year Rockefeller founded Standard Oil) to 5.9 cents per gallon in 1897 (the year Rockefeller retired from Standard). Rockefeller never once held a gun to anyone's head, much less dispatched goons and terrorists to kill untold numbers of innocent people.

The only people 'harmed' by Rockefeller were his competitors (such as Franklin Tarbell, father of Ida) who failed to keep up with Standard's innovations and cost-reducing techniques. Meanwhile, Rockefeller improved the lives of literally tens of millions of people.

The Qaddafis, in contrast, are thieving, tyrannical, and murderous brutes.

Sincerely,

Donald J. Boudreaux

Henry Wallace was the Progressive Party candidate for president in 1948. He believed that both the American and the Russian revolutions were part of "the march to freedom of the past 150 years." After having met Soviet Minister Molotov, Wallace arranged a trip to the "Wild East" of Russia. On May 23, 1944, he started a twenty-five-day journey accompanied by Owen Lattimore. They were hosted by generals of the NKVD, the Soviet secret police. The NKVD presented a fully sanitized version of the slave labor camps in Magadan and Kolyma to their American guests, convinced them that all the work was done by volunteers, charmed them with entertainment, and left their guests impressed with the "development" of Siberia and the spirit of the "volunteers." Lattimore's film of the visit tells that " a village . . . in Siberia is a forum for open discussion like a town meeting in New England."[17]

It is estimated that more than one million people died in the Soviet labor camps such as those that Wallace visited.

ORWELLIAN NEWSPEAK REACHES NEW HEIGHTS.

17 May 2010

Prof. Paul Krugman
Department of Economics
Princeton University

Dear Prof. Krugman:

In your May 14 blog post "Why Libertarianism Doesn't Work, Part N" you attempt to tar libertarianism as being an ideology that "requires incorruptible politicians."

You're deeply confused. One foundation of libertarianism is the observation that no profession is as infested with corruption as is politics.

The political ideology built upon the outlandish assumption that politicians are incorruptible and trustworthy isn't libertarianism but, rather, your own—namely, "Progressivism." You and your ilk unceasingly plead for politicians to be entrusted with ever-more power and money, while libertarians—understanding that politicians aren't the saints that you presume them to be—oppose your efforts.

Your accusing libertarianism of requiring "incorruptible politicians" makes as much sense as a faith-healer accusing science-based medicine of requiring competent witch-doctors.

Sincerely,

Donald Boudreaux

Soviet tanks invade the streets of Budapest, Hungary, in 1956 after the people demanded freedom.

New York Stock Exchange open for trade, 1955

COMMUNISM AND CAPITALISM.

9 November 2009

Editor, The New York Times
620 Eighth Avenue
New York, NY 10018

To the Editor:

Slavoj Zizek rightly complains—if with understatement bordering on the vulgar—of being "deceived" by communism ("20 Years of Collapse," Nov. 9). But like many other pundits who feign wisdom by steering clear of what they mistakenly interpret to be an extreme position, he complains also of being "disillusioned" by capitalism.

Capitalism is indeed poles apart from communism, but not in a way that renders society best served by some compromise between the two. Unlike communism and milder forms of collectivism, capitalism is not imposed; it is simply what arises when adults are free to engage in consensual commercial acts in cultures that respect private property rights and largely reject both status and superstition as guides to decision-making. Also unlike communism, capitalism conscripts no one to serve other persons' ends; individuals can opt out of capitalist societies.

Perhaps most importantly, unlike communism, capitalism promises neither to produce heaven on earth nor to engineer any New and Better Man—and so capitalism gives rise to none of the murderous zealotry endemic to communism.

Sincerely,

Donald J. Boudreaux

Regarded as one of the most influential American literary critics of the first half of the twentieth century, H. L. Mencken criticized writers who he felt were fraudulently successful and promoted the work of lesser-known newcomers like Theodore Dreiser and Sinclair Lewis. A fierce proponent of individualism, he was known as the "Sage of Baltimore" and often used his literary criticism and journalistic writing to take jabs at American social and cultural weaknesses: pretension, provincialism, Christian radicalism, and the "booboisie"— the uncultured, unthinking middle class of America.

READING BENJAMIN BARBER REMINDS ME OF READING THORSTEIN VEBLEN, AND OF MENCKEN'S QUESTION AFTER HE'D READ THAT "GREAT GEYSER OF PISHPOSH": "WHAT WAS THE SWEATING PROFESSOR TRYING TO SAY?"

....

15 April 2007

Editor, Baltimore Sun
501 N. Calvert Street
Baltimore, Maryland 21278

To the Editor:

Benjamin Barber laments the great diversity and abundance of products available in modern market economies ("Overselling capitalism with consumerism," April 15). His lamentation reaches its crescendo when he proclaims that "When we see politics permeate every sector of life, we call it totalitarianism. When religion rules all, we call it theocracy. But when commerce dominates everything, we call it liberty."

He compares rifles to roses. Totalitarianism and theocracy are evil because, under them, persons with power bend innocent people to their will though the use of violence. Commerce is the opposite. It is a peaceful series of voluntary offers to buy and to sell. It *is* liberty—and it is profoundly good.

Sincerely,

★ ★ ★

"We will be able to look back and tell our children that this was the moment when we began to provide care for the sick and good jobs to the jobless; this was the moment when the rise of the oceans began to slow and our planet began to heal."

—Candidate Barack Obama after winning the Democratic nomination for president in 2008

HE SET THE STANDARD.

27 April 2011

Editor, Washington Post
1150 15th St., NW
Washington, DC 20071

Dear Editor:

Stephen Stromberg is correct that the recent run-up in gasoline prices isn't the fault of President Obama ("President Obama says that gas prices reflect supply and demand," April 27). But Mr. Stromberg is wrong to pity Mr. Obama for nevertheless being blamed by the public for their pain at the pumps.

Mr. Obama, like so many elected officials, won office by deluding voters with a grand image of a government that, in the right hands, can fix nearly every problem that troubles the good people of this republic—a government that can fix all that is broken, can cure all social ills (and many physical ones, too), and can transform this vale of trade-offs, scarcities, chance, and imperfections into a paradise in which the only suffering is that of Evil Villains finally brought to justice for the depredations that they've for so long inflicted upon the pure, noble, all-deserving We the People.

Because Mr. Obama assured us that with him at the helm Uncle Sam's powers to "change" society would be vast and amazing, he deserves no pity for being held accountable for his inability to perform the marvels that he promised to perform.

Sincerely,

If Congress can't fix things here, what makes you think they can fix things overseas?

GOVERNMENTS CAN BE BUILT; NATIONS MIGHT BE BUILT; CIVIL SOCIETIES, ALAS, CAN NEVER BE BUILT. THEY MUST EMERGE.

••

23 February 2011

Editor, Washington Post
1150 15th St., NW
Washington, DC 20071

Dear Editor:

William Kristol argues that "American principles" require Uncle Sam to intervene more vigorously—with force, if necessary—in the revolutions now sweeping through the Middle East ("Obama's moment in the Middle East—and at home," Feb. 23).

I disagree. While we should cheer for liberalization to grow and spread throughout the Middle East, American principles counsel our government *not* to interfere. One of these principles, after all, is that government (even our own) is an inherently dangerous agent best kept on as short a leash as possible. Another of these principles is that top-down social engineering is bound to have undesirable unintended consequences—a fact that is no less true when the social engineers are headquartered in the Pentagon and the State Department as when they are headquartered in the Department of Health and Human Services and the Department of Education. The same government that Mr. Kristol so often, and rightly, criticizes for making a mess of matters here at home is unlikely to become a shining example of efficiency, rectitude, and Solomaic wisdom in foreign lands.

Sincerely,

Donald J. Boudreaux

★　★　★

The estimated annual revenue for the illegal drug industry worldwide ranges from $45 to $280 billion. The 2012 federal budget is $3.7 trillion. The entire U.S. sports industry is estimated to be $422 billion.[18]

OUR LEADERS:
HTTP://MEXIDATA.INFO/ID2931.HTML

• •

11 February 2011

Secretary Hillary Clinton
U.S. Department of State
Washington, DC

Dear Ms. Clinton:

When asked by a Mexican journalist if drug legalization is a good idea you replied "It is not likely to work. There is just too much money in it."

Overlooking the fact that much of the money in the illegal-drug trade is there only because those drugs are illegal, do you also believe that, say, professional American football should be illegal? The N.F.L. and its players make a *lot* of money!

What about coffee? In 2010, Starbucks revenue alone was nearly $11 billion. And how about currently legal over-the-counter medicines— plenty of money in *that* trade! Annual aspirin sales globally are more than $1 billion, and that's on top of all the money made by selling the likes of acetaminophen, ibuprofen, various antihistamines, and Flintstones vitamins.

If, however, you're right that it's best to outlaw enterprises in which there "is just too much money," then surely we must forthwith criminalize government. The money that is "in" Uncle Sam alone dwarfs the sums exchanged in the market for illegal drugs.

Sincerely,

FRIEDMAN AND KENNEDY.

20 January 2011

Editor, Washington Post
1150 15th St., NW
Washington, DC 20071

Dear Editor:

Unlike E.J. Dionne, I neither admire nor find inspiration in JFK's famous line "Ask not what your country can do for you—ask what you can do for your country" ("Kennedy's inaugural address presents a challenge still," Jan. 20). The late Milton and Rose Friedman explained best why that statement is detestable:

"Neither half of the statement expresses a relation between the citizen and his government that is worthy of the ideals of free men in a free society. The paternalistic 'what your country can do for you' implies that government is the patron, the citizen the ward, a view that is at odds with the free man's belief in his own responsibility for his own destiny. The organismic, 'what you can do for your 'country' implies the government is the master or the deity, the citizen, the servant or the votary."[19]

Free men and women abhor the very thought of being either wards or servants of the state, and are not charmed out of this attitude by soaring slogans.

Sincerely,

[signature]

"My share of the U.S. debt is *how* much? Can one-year-olds file for bankruptcy?"

HYPOCRITES.
....

8 January 2011

Editor, The Wall Street Journal
1211 6th Ave.
New York, NY 10036

To the Editor:

Paul Luce rightly notes that new legislation limiting the issuance of credit by retail stores is obnoxiously paternalistic: many customers who wish to buy on credit, and many retailers who wish to take the risk of extending credit, are now arbitrarily prevented from doing so (Letters, Jan. 8).

This legislation is especially infuriating because the same politicians who voted for it—the very same officious intermeddlers who claim to care so deeply about protecting unsuspecting Americans from being burdened with excessive debt—wantonly and routinely foist huge debt burdens on each and every American (and our progeny) through Uncle Sam's soaring budget deficits.

What kind of twisted mind thinks it to be acceptable to load debt onto someone unilaterally—without that person's consent—but unacceptable to allow that same person to choose his or her own level of debt burden?

Sincerely,

Thomas Edison, John Burroughs, and Henry Ford

Henry Ford (July 30, 1863–April 7, 1947) was a prominent American industrialist, the founder of the Ford Motor Company, and sponsor of the development of the assembly line technique of mass production. His introduction of the Model T automobile revolutionized transportation and American industry. As owner of the Ford Motor Company, he became one of the richest and best-known people in the world. He is credited with "Fordism": mass production of inexpensive goods coupled with high wages for workers. Ford had a global vision, with consumerism as the key to peace. His intense commitment to systematically lowering costs resulted in many technical and business innovations, including a franchise system that put dealerships throughout most of North America and in major cities on six continents.[20]

IT'S THE CONSUMER, STUPID.

14 October 2008

Editor, The Wall Street Journal
200 Liberty Street
New York, NY 10281

To the Editor:

In her otherwise fine essay "A Capitalist Manifesto" (Oct. 13), Judy Shelton claims that capitalism "accords primacy to the entrepreneur."

Not true. Capitalism accords primacy to the consumer. While capitalism rewards entrepreneurs who succeed, success under capitalism is defined as pleasing consumers. Capitalism does not, and should not, tolerate entrepreneurs who don't satisfy consumers.

The system that gives primacy to the entrepreneur—or at least to prominent producers—is corporatism. Government interventions such as tariffs accord primacy to the producer and, as a result, move us away from capitalism and toward corporatism.

Sincerely,

"The Lord's Prayer is 66 words; the
Gettysburg address is 286 words; there
are 1,322 words in the Declaration of
Independence, but government regulations
on the sale of cabbage total 26,911 words."

—David McIntosh, *National Review*

(Being *that* inefficient is an achievement.)

IT'S A MAGIC SHOW IN WHICH THE RABBIT FAILS TO SPRING FROM THE HAT BUT IN WHICH SOME AUDIENCE MEMBERS REALLY DO GET SAWED IN HALF.

....

22 September 2010

Editor, Washington Post
1150 15th St., NW
Washington, DC 20071

Dear Editor:

Dana Milbank thinks the Democrats aren't sufficiently boastful ("Do-nothing Democrats," Sept. 22). He writes that "Over the past 20 months, Democrats have done a lot—too much, the opposition says. But they don't want to talk about the achievements. The stimulus bill is unpopular; they're not getting credit for health-care legislation, financial reforms and many other accomplishments."

Enacting legislation is neither an "achievement" nor an "accomplishment" that, standing alone, deserves credit. To think otherwise is akin to thinking that a rain-dancer deserves credit for performing his fancy ritual even if afterward the crops continue to wilt because the drought persists.

Sincerely,

[signature]

★　★　★

"Competition is the final price
determinant and competitive prices
may result in profits which force you
to accept a rate of return less than you
hoped for, or for that matter to accept
temporary losses."

—Alfred P. Sloan, President, CEO, and/or
Chairman of General Motors from 1923-1956

I'VE SAID IT BEFORE: TRYING TO LEARN ECONOMICS FROM THE POPULAR MEDIA IS LIKE TRYING TO LEARN PHYSICS BY WATCHING ROAD RUNNER CARTOONS.

31 March 2008

Director, Fox News
1211 Avenue of the Americas
New York, NY 10036

Dear Sir or Madam:

Fox Morning News co-host Megyn Kelly naively worries that Pernod's acquisition of Vin & Spirit AB (maker of Absolut vodka) will lead to higher prices paid by those of us who belly up to the bar (March 31). Ms. Kelly reasons that, because many analysts regard the $8 billion paid by Pernod for Vin & Spirit to be "too high," Pernod will raise the prices it charges for its products in order to recover the losses it would otherwise suffer as a result of paying such a large sum for Vin & Spirit.

If Ms. Kelly's economics were correct, bankruptcies would be unknown. Any business finding its revenues to be inadequate would simply raise the prices it charges for its products and enjoy the resulting higher revenues. Any individual finding his income too low would simply demand a higher wage and enjoy his resulting higher income. If covering expenses were as easy as simply demanding higher prices for whatever it is you sell, then we'd all live in a bizarre economic paradise—one in which it would be meaningless to describe anyone as paying "too much" for an asset or as living beyond his means.

Sincerely,

Donald J. Boudreaux

Deregulated coffee markets have brought a peace dividend to Africa.
Drink up!

DOUX COMMERCE.

· ·

19 February 2008

Editor, The Washington Times
3600 New York Ave NE
Washington, DC 20002

Dear Editor:

Reflecting on Rwanda's gruesome 1994 genocide, President Bush correctly noted that "evil does exist" ("Bush honors Rwandan dead," February 19). But Rwanda's post-genocide experience teaches a lesson that remains too-little appreciated: commerce crowds out evil.

My wife, Karol Boudreaux, has done extensive research in Rwanda. She finds compelling evidence that Rwanda's deregulation of its coffee market has played a major role in calming tribal hostilities in that country.[21] With commercial opportunities in the very large coffee industry now more widely available than before, Hutus and Tutsis, who just a few years ago sought to slaughter each other, now mutually prosper by working side by side to grow and process coffee for the global market.

Commerce, not arms, brought peace and the seeds of prosperity to Rwanda.

Sincerely,

[signature: Donald J. Boudreaux]

WANNA BET THAT ORSZAG AND DEPARLE WILL BE PROVEN WRONG—SAY, BY 2030? SERIOUSLY, WANNA BET?

....

5 March 2010

Editor, Washington Post
1150 15th St., NW
Washington, DC 20071

Dear Editor:

Administration officials Peter Orszag and Nancy-Ann DeParle try to assure us that Obamacare is "health reform that won't break the bank" (March 5). While Mr. Orszag and Ms. DeParle have undoubtedly worked with great care on all of their cost estimates, I remain skeptical: on Wednesday, David Harsanyi reported in the *Denver Post* that "Congress estimated Medicare's cost at $12 billion for 1990 (adjusted for inflation) when the program kicked off in 1965. Medicare cost $107 billion in 1990 and is quickly approaching $500 billion."[22]

So, because the inflation-adjusted, actual cost of Medicare during its first quarter-century of operation overran its projected cost by 700 percent (!), Mr. Orszag and Ms. DeParle must forgive those of us who aren't comforted by their insistence that Obamacare is fiscally sound.

Sincerely,

"Slavery is Freedom"

—George Orwell, *1984*

THE LOGIC, I SUPPOSE, IS THAT WE SHOULD BE FREE TO DO ONLY WHAT IS WISE AND GOOD AND APPROVED BY ELITE OPINION.

••

10 December 2006

The Editor, New York Times
229 West 43rd St.
New York, NY 10036

To the Editor:

Writing in support of NYC's ban on trans fats, Dr. Soja John Thaikattil (Letters, Dec. 10) argues that "Experience has shown that consumers do not always use their freedom to make healthy choices. So a regulation that is based on science and in the best interests of the consumer should not be interpreted as an unwarranted intrusion into personal lifestyle choices. Is the freedom to choose unhealthy food that difficult to forfeit?"

Suppose NYC had banned newspapers from reporting on controversial issues. I wonder if Dr. Thaikattil would then write "Experience has shown that newspapers do not always use their freedom to report wisely. So a regulation that is based on science and in the best interest of the public should not be interpreted as an unwarranted intrusion into freedom of the press. Is the freedom to report unwisely that difficult to forfeit?"

Sincerely,

Used with permission of *National Review*

HAT TIP TO WALTER WILLIAMS.

7 March 2010

Editor, The New York Times
620 Eighth Avenue
New York, NY 10018

To the Editor:

Paul Krugman says that the idea that unemployment benefits reduce people's incentives to find jobs is "bizarre" and at odds with "textbook economics" ("Senator Bunning's Universe," March 5).

Prof. Krugman must count himself and his wife among those who hold bizarre ideas—or who, when writing economics textbooks, misrepresent economists' views. Here's what they wrote on page 210 of their jointly authored textbook *Macroeconomics* (2nd ed.), published in 2009: "Public policy designed to help workers who lose their jobs can lead to structural unemployment as an unintended side effect . . . . In other countries, particularly in Europe, benefits are more generous and last longer. The drawback to this generosity is that it reduces a worker's incentive to quickly find a new job. Generous unemployment benefits in some European countries are widely believed to be one of the main causes of 'Eurosclerosis,' the persistent high unemployment that affects a number of European countries."

Sincerely,

Donald J. Boudreaux

"Debts have to be repaid, not trade deficits."

THIS KICKABLE HORSE WON'T DIE.

29 July 2008

Editor, New York Sun
105 Chambers Street
New York, NY 10007

Dear Editor:

Usually sure-footed, Martin Feldstein stumbles when he argues that "America will need a trade surplus" in order to "repay" today's trade deficit ("Thinking About the Dollar," July 28). First, the only part of the trade deficit that must be repaid is the part that becomes debt, such as when foreigners buy Treasury notes. When foreigners buy dollar-denominated equity or real estate, or when they make greenfield investments in the U.S. or simply hold dollars, no debt is created. None of these investments require repayment.

Second, when it comes to repaying debt, the trade deficit is a red herring. It matters not if a creditor is an American or an Armenian: the debt must be repaid and, if repaid in dollars, those dollars will eventually be redeemed for American goods, services, or assets. (The last could put upward pressure on America's trade deficit.) Uncle Sam and many private Americans might well have financed excessive consumption with excessive debt, but, if so, the problem is the debt and not the nationalities of the creditors.

Sincerely,

Income Mobility for Lower Income Groups from 1996 to 2005

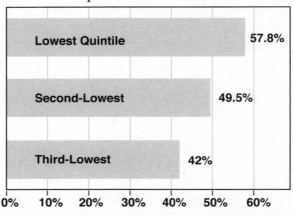

Percent Moving to a Higher Income Group by 2005

Graph reproduced from the Carpe Diem blog with the kind permission of Mark Perry.
Data are from Thomas A. Garrett, "U.S. Income Inequality: It's Not So Bad," *In the Vault*,
Federal Reserve Bank of St. Louis, Spring 2010:
http//www.stlouisfed.org/publications/itv/articles/?id=1920

MORE AND MORE MIDDLE-CLASS AMERICANS ARE DISAPPEARING—INTO THE UPPER CLASSES. (AND WITH APOLOGIES TO ARNOLD KLING.)

19 October 2007

The Editor, New York Times
620 Eighth Avenue
New York, NY 10018

To the Editor:

Judith Warner writes that "More and more people are being priced out of a middle class existence" ("The Clinton Surprise," October 19). This statement is true, but only because more and more Americans are getting richer. Consider the percentage of American households in each of these different annual-income categories in 1967 and in 2003 (all reckoned in 2003 dollars):

	1967	2003
$75K and up	8.2	26.1
$50K–$75K	16.7	18.0
$35K–$50K	22.3	15.0
$15K–$35K	31.1	25.0
under $15K	21.7	15.9

If the middle class is disappearing, it's doing so by swelling the ranks of the upper classes.

Sincerely,

[signature]

Making a molehill into a mountain

DISPOSING OF A MYTH.
....

26 June 2008

Editor, Washington Times
3600 New York Ave NE
Washington, DC 20002

Dear Editor:

In his letter of June 26, Andy Arnold writes as if Americans are running out of space to use as garbage landfills.

Rubbish.

Clemson University economist Daniel Benjamin, in a 2004 paper prepared for the environmental research organization PERC, reports that "The United States today has more landfill capacity than ever before . . . Given that the total land area needed to hold all of America's garbage for the next century would be only about 10 miles on a side, it is safe to conclude that far more rubbish than is worth considering will fit into far less area than is worth worrying about."[23]

Sincerely,

[signature]

Milton Friedman with his wife, Rose, receiving the 1976 Nobel Prize
for Economics. Photo courtesy of Free To Choose Enterprise.

ALTHOUGH REVIEWED IN THE *WASHINGTON POST BOOK WORLD'S* "ECONOMICS" SECTION, NAOMI KLEIN'S BOOK IS TO ECONOMICS WHAT SPIDERMAN COMIC BOOKS ARE TO ARACHNOLOGY.

25 November 2007

Editor, Washington Post
1150 15th St., NW
Washington, DC 20071

Dear Editor:

In her new book, Naomi Klein reveals what she sees as a smoking gun in the hands of the late Milton Friedman. It's true that Mr. Friedman wrote that "only a crisis—actual or perceived—produces real change" ("Doing Well by Doing Ill," November 25). From these words Ms. Klein draws the fantastically mistaken conclusion that Mr. Friedman was summoning capitalists to wreak havoc upon an unsuspecting world. Unfortunately, reviewer Shashi Tharoor's defense of Mr. Friedman—that he should not be read literally—also misses the point.

Ms. Klein's mistake is the sophomoric one of confusing description with prescription. Mr. Friedman's claim was descriptive. It is of the same genre as the claim made to my family years ago by a physician who shared our frustration at my overweight father's refusal to eat a healthier diet: "It'll likely take a heart attack to convince him to eat less and exercise more." If Ms. Klein had heard this statement, I suspect that she would have warned us that my dad's doctor was prescribing for him a heart attack!

Sincerely,

[signature]

SELF-DELUSION IS ONE THING; TRYING TO PERSUADE OTHERS THAT YOUR SELF-DELUSIONS ARE REALISTIC IS QUITE ANOTHER.

....

16 March 2009

Editor, Baltimore Sun
501 N. Calvert Street
Baltimore, Maryland 21278

Dear Editor:

Opposing merit pay for teachers, retired teacher Jim Apgar claims that he and his colleagues were motivated only by their students' needs and that "no amount of money would have improved my performance" (Letters, March 16).

Wow! Taking Mr. Apgar at his word implies that no *reduction* in the amount of money he was paid would have *worsened* his performance. Indeed, his claim suggests that he would have continued to teach—and teach well—even if his employer had stopped paying him altogether.

If Mr. Apgar is both truthful and representative of teachers, cash-strapped school districts can stop worrying and simply slash teachers' pay dramatically.

Sincerely,

Donald J. Boudreaux

Farming has its risks and its rewards. None should be government guaranteed.

THERE IS NO POLICY, NO MATTER HOW EXTRAVAGANTLY RAPACIOUS, THAT CANNOT FIND SOME IGNORAMUS TO TRY TO JUSTIFY IT AS BEING NECESSARY AND EVEN ENLIGHTENED.

....

17 December 2007

Editor, The Wall Street Journal
200 Liberty Street
New York, NY 10281

To the Editor:

Trying to justify government support of agriculture, Gary Owens asserts that before Uncle Sam started milking taxpayers for the benefit of farmers, "if weather or disease interfered with yields, [a farmer's] only option was to borrow again and try the following year."

Not so. Farmers could buy insurance from private cooperatives and companies.

It's appalling that so much of the popular sympathy for government support of farmers is founded on myths, superstitions, and plain ignorance.

Sincerely,

[signature: Donald J. Boudreaux]

Clara Barton, founder of the Red Cross, didn't need government programs or regulations to demonstrate her compassion.

WINNING AN ARGUMENT IS EASY IF YOU ASSUME THAT THE RELEVANT CONCLUSION IN SUPPORT OF YOUR ARGUMENT IS TRUE.

· ·

22 May 2011

Editor, Los Angeles Times
202 West 1st Street
Los Angeles, California 90012

Dear Editor:

Discussing the past 30 years, Neal Gabler asserts that "Conservatives are pushing aside compassion" ("America the stony-hearted," May 22). In doing so, though, he simply *assumes* his conclusion—namely, that a people's compassion is expressed only, or at least best, through government programs and regulations.

Conservatives (or, more accurately here, skeptics of the welfare state) argue that government programs, because these rely upon taxation and force, are not the product of a people's compassion. These are instead the product of force-backed greed masquerading as compassion (Ever reflect on why the Food Stamp program is run by the Department of Agriculture, or why labor unions oppose free trade?), as well as of the wide acceptance of the myth that society and state are synonymous with each other.

We welfare-state skeptics might or might not be wrong that true compassion can be expressed only when done voluntarily and that, when compassion is done voluntarily, it's more effective than is 'compassion' compelled by government commands. But Mr. Gabler is certainly wrong to write as if the argument on this front is settled in favor of those who suppose that a people's compassion can be expressed only through the state.

Sincerely,

Dignified?

YOU WANT TO SEE THE OPPOSITE OF DIGNITY?

....

11 July 2009
Editor, The New York Times
620 Eighth Avenue
New York, NY 10018

To the Editor:

Morton Winkel agrees with David Brooks's assessment that capitalism destroys dignity (Letters, July 11).

There are many reasons to reject this fatuous conclusion. But because I write this letter from Tbilisi, Georgia, I report personally one such reason visible to anyone here. This city is crowded with hideously ugly, dilapidated, and spirit-devastating concrete buildings erected by the Soviets. Living and working in these overgrown hovels is anything but dignified. In vivid contrast to the impersonal communist-era structures are the buildings and homes built since the fall of the Soviet Union. These structures—products of powerful doses of capitalist creativity, enterprise, and consumer choice—are warm, unique, personal, attractive, and functional.

Dignity is destroyed, not by capitalism, but by the heavy-handed and arrogant state.

Sincerely,

Outcomes of Market vs. Monopoly School Systems, Number of Significant and Insignificant Findings

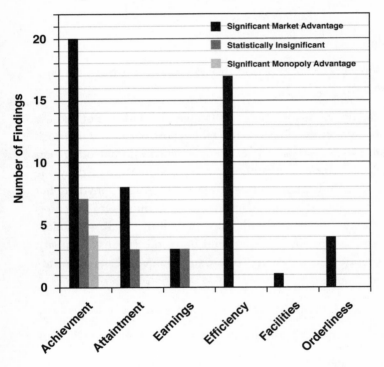

Source: Andrew J. Coulson (2009), "Comparing Public, Private, and Market Schools: The International Evidence," *Journal of School Choice*, vol. 3, no.1, 31-54.

ANSWER ME THIS.
··········

25 April 2011

Editor, The Wall Street Journal
1211 6th Ave.
New York, NY 10036

Dear Editor:

Randi Weingarten insists that "markets aren't the education solution" (April 25). Let's see. Suppose groceries were supplied in the same way that K-12 education is supplied.

People would pay property taxes. Government would spend these tax receipts on building and operating supermarkets. Each household would be assigned to a particular supermarket from which it would get its weekly allotment of groceries for "free." (Department of Supermarket officials would determine the quantities and kinds of groceries that families are entitled to receive.) Each family would be allowed to patronize only that "public" supermarket to which it is assigned.

Residents of wealthier counties would obviously have better-stocked supermarkets than would residents of poorer counties. Indeed, the quality of public supermarkets would play a major role in determining people's choices of neighborhoods in which to live.

When the quality of supermarkets becomes widely recognized to be dismal, calls for "supermarket choice" would arise, only to be ridiculed as a right-wing ploy to deny ordinary families the ability to eat. Such choice, it would be alleged, would drain resources from public supermarkets whose poor performance *proves* that these supermarkets are underfunded.

Does anyone believe that such a system for supplying groceries would work well? Surely not. So why do so many people presume that government-supplied schooling is superior to market-supplied schooling?

Sincerely,

Donald J. Boudreaux

Wealthy plutocrats use devious means to steal money from the peasants.

CONTROL YOUR PRESUMPTIONS.
∙∙∙

20 November 2010

The Editor, The Economist.com
25 St James's Street
London SW1A 1HG
United Kingdom

Dear Sir:

Will Wilkinson's essay on income inequality in America is splendid ("This ain't no banana republic," Nov. 19). In it, Mr Wilkinson correctly challenges *New York Times* columnist Nicholas Kristof's claim that "the wealthiest plutocrats now actually control a greater share of the pie in the United States" than in several countries of Latin America. Rich Americans, Mr Wilkinson rightly points out, overwhelmingly are business people who serve the middle-classes and not political, military, or ecclesiastic predators who steal from peasants.

This fact makes Mr Kristof's claim that wealth is "controlled" in America highly misleading.

Except insofar as rich Americans succeed at getting government to protect their wealth with special privileges, such as tariffs, wealth is not "controlled." Wealth is created only by serving consumers—that is, by making others wealthier—and it flees from those who stop serving consumers. Should Apple stop producing innovative products that consumers willingly buy, Steve Jobs's fortune will disappear. Should Southwest Airlines start charging uncompetitive fares, its shareholders' wealth will dissolve. Should a super-wealthy hedge-fund manager consistently fail to increase the value of his clients' portfolio, he will become a not-so-super-wealthy ex-fund-manager.

In market economies, wealth isn't controlled so much as it is deployed in the service of others.

Sincerely,

[signature]

It's not hard to burn a straw man of your own making.

ONE OF THE FIRST THINGS I TEACH MY FRESHMEN CLASSES IS THAT INTENTIONS ARE NOT RESULTS.

· ·

19 December 2010

Editor, Los Angeles Times
202 West 1st Street
Los Angeles, California 90012

Dear Editor:

Tom Lutz is probably correct that Rep. John Boehner's much-publicized weepings are trashy political theatrics ("A crying shame," Dec. 16). But Mr. Lutz is incorrect to assert that it is a "deep contradiction" to claim to care about children while being against government programs such as "health insurance for children, . . . against unemployment benefits, against equal pay, against food safety, against money for teachers, against raising the minimum wage, against tobacco education, mine safety, alternative energy, pollution control, whistle-blower protection, science and technology research."

To oppose government provision of such things is not to be "against" such things. Nearly everyone wants every American to have adequate insurance, safe foods, high pay, affordable health care, and all the other advantages of modern commercial society. But many of us reject Mr. Lutz's assumption that these benefits can be provided only (or best) by government.

Maybe those of us who argue that ordinary people will be more prosperous and secure with less government are mistaken. But as long as Mr. Lutz and other "Progressives" continue to impute sordid motives to persons who wish to rein in the state, they disadvantage themselves politically by failing to understand their opponents.

Sincerely,

Donald Boudreaux

WHACK-A-MOLE:
HTTP://BUYAMERICANCHALLENGE.WORDPRESS.COM/2011/02/12/
RECORD-CRUSHED-U-S-TRADE-DEFICIT-WITH-CHINA-273-BILLION-
IN-2010-BIGGEST-EVER-BETWEEN-TWO-COUNTRIES/
••

13 February 2011
Mr. Randy Erwin
Buy America Challenge blog

Dear Mr. Erwin:

Thanks for exporting to my household your blog post "Record Crushed: U.S. Trade Deficit with China—$273 Billion in 2010—Biggest Ever Between Two Countries." You write there that "We can solve our country's economic problem ourselves by changing our buying habits just slightly and buying American more often. The average adult consumes $700 per month in imported goods. If we could reduce that to $517 per person per month, we would have no trade deficit at all. With no trade deficit, we would likely have 3-4% unemployment. All we need to do is reduce our consumption of imported goods 25% to have jobs again in this country. That will secure our long-term economic future."

I've some questions for you.

—Because "buying American more often" means rejecting lower-priced imports for higher-priced American goods, we'll have less money to spend at the movies, at restaurants, and the like. How do you know that the job losses from contractions in these industries won't offset whatever job gains emerge elsewhere from "buying American more often"?

—At least half of all U.S. imports are inputs used by American firms. So if American firms substitute more costly American-made inputs for lower-priced imported inputs, American firms' costs will rise. They'll then lose market share. Might the job losses that result from these firms' contractions and bankruptcies offset whatever job gains emerge from "buying American more often"?

Sincerely,

Donald Boudreaux

219

Photo by Theodore H. Mock Photography

Thomas Sowell, born in North Carolina and raised in Harlem, left home early, without finishing high school. He later joined the Marine Corps and became a photographer in the Korean War. When his service concluded, Sowell began studying economics while attending Harvard University and continuing part-time photography work. He graduated magna cum laude from Harvard, later receiving a master's in economics from Columbia University and a doctorate in economics from the University of Chicago.

Over the course of his career, Sowell has published a dozen books, in addition to many articles and essays, which cover everything from classical economic theory to choosing the right college, from civil rights to judicial activism.

THE CLOSING SENTENCE IN SOWELL'S 1980 BOOK, *KNOWLEDGE & DECISIONS:* "FREEDOM IS NOT SIMPLY THE RIGHT OF INTELLECTUALS TO CIRCULATE THEIR MERCHANDISE. IT IS, ABOVE ALL, THE RIGHT OF ORDINARY PEOPLE TO FIND ELBOW ROOM FOR THEMSELVES AND A REFUGE FROM THE RAMPAGING PRESUMPTIONS OF THEIR 'BETTERS.'"

• •

25 October 2010

Editor, The New York Times Book Review
620 Eighth Avenue
New York, NY 10018

To the Editor:

A theme that runs with approval throughout Jonathan Alter's review of recent books on modern "liberalism" is that "liberals," in contrast to their mindless Cro-Magnon opposites, overflow with ideas ("The State of Liberalism," Oct. 24).

Indeed they do. But these ideas are almost exclusively about how other people should live their lives. These are ideas about how one group of people (the politically successful) should engineer everyone else's contracts, social relations, diets, habits, and even moral sentiments.

Put differently, modern "liberalism's" ideas are about replacing an unimaginably large multitude of diverse and competing ideas—each one individually chosen, practiced, assessed, and modified in light of what F.A. Hayek called "the particular circumstances of time and place"—with a relatively paltry set of 'Big Ideas' that are politically selected, centrally imposed, and enforced not by the natural give, take, and compromise of the everyday interactions of millions of people but, rather, by guns wielded by those whose overriding 'idea' is among the most simple-minded and antediluvian notions in history, namely, that those with the power of the sword are anointed to lord it over the rest of us.

Sincerely,

Donald J. Boudreaux

Whose restaurant do you want to eat in?

I DIDN'T GO THERE IN MY LETTER, BUT I DO WONDER IF THIS RESTAURATEUR'S COMPETITORS ARE LESS ABLE THAN SHE IS TO ABSORB THE COSTS OF THIS LEGISLATION.

· ·

30 July 2011

Editor, The Wall Street Journal
1211 6th Ave.
New York, NY 10036

Dear Editor:

Preferring to extract conclusions from her personal experience, San Francisco restaurateur Jennifer Piallat explicitly rejects the use of a "barrage of statistics" to analyze the consequences of legislation that mandates paid sick-leave for employees (Letters, July 30). And in Ms. Piallat's experience, legislation mandating paid sick-leave improves firms' performances. The anecdote she offers from her own restaurant is that, since the legislation went into effect, employees no longer report to work while sick and, hence, no longer infect fellow employees with their ailments.

I don't doubt the truth of Ms. Piallat's account. But it begs the question: why did she not offer paid sick-leave to her employees on her own? If paid sick-leave increases her restaurant's bottom line by, as she says, improving her staffs' performance, why did she wait to be forced by politicians to adopt that policy?

Perhaps she just didn't think of doing so, or perhaps she's a poor businesswoman. Whatever the reason, Ms. Piallat's personal experience is hardly justification for substituting the business judgment of people who specialize in winning political office for that of people who specialize in actually running businesses in competitive markets.

Sincerely,

Annual Public School Spending
Per Pupil and Percent Change in
Achievement of 17-Year-Olds Since 1970

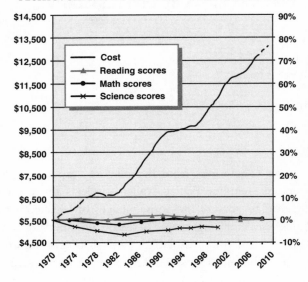

Cato Institute

Data Source (cost):
Digest of Education
Statistics 2009, Table
182, CPI adjusted
to constant 2010$.
Missing values
linearly interpolated
or extrapolated.

(scores): NAEP Long
Term Trends reports.

Prepared by:
Andrew J. Coulson,
Director, Cato
Institute Center for
Educational Freedom

Percent Change in Public School
Employment and Enrollment Since 1970

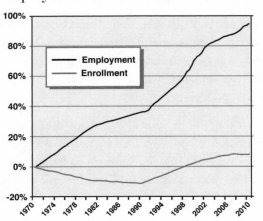

Cato Institute

Data Source:
National Center for
Education Statistics,
*Digest of Education
Statistics 2010* (April,
2011), Tables 35, 36,
84. Missing Values
linearly interpolated
or extrapolated.

Prepared by:
Andrew J. Coulson,
Director, Cato
Institute Center for
Educational Freedom

The skyrocketing cost and employment levels of public schools are
matched by remarkably flat student scores and enrollment.

OVERLOOK KRISTOF'S DUBIOUS PREMISE THAT MONEY IS THE MOST IMPORTANT KEY TO GOOD EDUCATION.

··

17 July 2011

Editor, The New York Times
620 Eighth Avenue
New York, NY 10018

Dear Editor:

Writing ominously that "All across America, school budgets are being cut, teachers laid off and education programs dismantled," Nicholas Kristof accuses us Americans of recklessly endangering our future ("Our Broken Escalator," July 17).

Context calms these fears.

While Mr. Kristof is correct that "70 percent of school districts nation-wide endured budget cuts in the school year that just ended, and 84 percent anticipate cuts this year," a quick web check reveals that these cuts average no more than about five percent. Further, these cuts overwhelmingly reflect simply the completion of the distribution of the $100 billion in federal 'stimulus' funds shoveled from Washington to state school systems in 2009-2010.

More broadly, data from the U.S. Department of Education's National Center for Education Statistics show that inflation-adjusted *per-pupil* expenditures for K-12 public schools have steadily and dramatically increased over the past half-century. In 2007-08 (just before the recession and the 'stimuli') real per-pupil funding was 19 percent higher than in 1999-2000, 33 percent higher than in 1990-91, 83 percent higher than in 1980-81, 129 percent higher than in 1970-71, and 272 percent higher than in 1961-62.[24]

Mr. Kristof's portrayal of the funding of K-12 schooling in America is recklessly uninformed.

Sincerely,

According to Professor Morici, these homeowners are extremely lucky.

WHADDYA THINK? $25 BUCKS AN HOUR?

29 August 2011

Prof. Peter Morici
University of Maryland
Smith School of Business
College Park, MD 20742-1815

Dear Peter:

In your blog-post yesterday at CNBC you argue that the destruction caused by hurricane Irene will spark a "process of economic renewal [that] can leave communities better off than before" ("Economic Impact of Hurricane Irene"). Central to your argument is your claim that, because of the rebuilding, "the capital stock that emerges will prove more economically useful and productive."

In other words, whenever assets still in use are destroyed, the owners of those assets are made richer because these destroyed assets are replaced with ones that are newer and more productive.

I hereby offer my services to you, at a modest wage, to destroy your house and car. Act now, and I'll destroy at no extra charge of all of your clothing, furniture, computer hardware and software, and household appliances.

Because, I'm sure, almost all of these things that I'll destroy for you are more than a few days old (and, hence, are hampered by wear and tear), you'll be obliged to replace them with newer versions that are "more economically useful and productive." You will, by your own logic, be made richer.

Just send me a note with some times that are good for you for me to come by with some sledge hammers and blowtorches. Given the short distance between Fairfax and College Park, I can be at your place pronto.

Oh, as an extra bonus, I promise not to clean up the mess! That way, there'll be more jobs created for clean-up crews in your neighborhood.

Sincerely,

ENDNOTES
··············

1. Robert Higgs, *Competition and Coercion: Blacks in the American Economy 1865-1914* (Chicago: University of Chicago Press, 1976).

2. http://www.phrases.org.uk/meanings/tanstaafl.html

3. Richard M. Ebeling, "Marching to Bismarck's Drummer: The Origins of the Modern Welfare State," *The Freeman*, Jan. 2007: http://www.thefreemanonline.org/from-the-president/marching-to-bismarcks-drummer-the-origins-of-the-modern-welfare-state/

4. Adapted from David R. Henderson at http://www.econlib.org/library/Enc/bios/Smith.html

5. Solomon W. Polachek and Carlos Seiglie, "Trade, Peace and Democracy: An Analysis of Dyadic Dispute" (June 2006): http://papers.ssrn.com/sol3/papers.cfm?abstract_id=915360

6. Benn Steil and Manuel Hinds, *Money, Markets & Sovereignty* (New Haven: Yale University Press, 2009), p. 70.

7. http://econlog.econlib.org/archives/2009/01/the_stimulus_an.html

8. Data available here: http://www.weather.gov/om/hazstats.shtml

9. Wikipedia contributors, "William M. Tweed," Wikipedia, The Free Encyclopedia, http://en.wikipedia.org/w/index.php?title=William_M._Tweed&oldid=456365816 (accessed October 25, 2011).

10. (Washington, DC: Human Rights Watch, 2000). http://www.hrw.org/legacy/reports/2000/usa/Rcedrg00.htm#P54_1086

11. http://findarticles.com/p/articles/mi_m1568/is_n9_v25/ai_15143266/pg_6/

12. http://www.fff.org/freedom/1196f.asp

13. Deirdre N. McCloskey, *Bourgeois Dignity* (Chicago: University of Chicago Press, 2010), p. 63.

14. http://www.senate.gov/employment/po/positions.htm

15. http://brown.senate.gov/newsroom/press_releases/release/?id=d96728df-3b1c-49ab-8e12-b9207f758cdb

16. http://www.uh.edu/~dguo/glossary_of_terms_used.htm [BTW, "the correct term is "proved reserves," not "proven reserves."]

17. Adapted from Wikipedia contributors, "Henry A. Wallace," Wikipedia, The Free Encyclopedia, http://en.wikipedia.org/w/index.php?title=Henry_A._Wallace&oldid=455152553 (accessed October 25, 2011).

18. http://www.drugwardistortions.org/distortion19.htm

19. Milton and Rose Friedman, *Capitalism and Freedom* (University of Chicago Press, 1962), p. 1.

20. Wikipedia contributors, "Henry Ford," Wikipedia, The Free Encyclopedia, http://en.wikipedia.org/w/index.php?title=Henry_Ford&oldid=455566034 (accessed October 25, 2011).

21. http://www.enterpriseafrica.org/Publications/pubID.4402/pub_detail.asp

22. http://www.denverpost.com/harsanyi/ci_14500665

23. http://www.environnement-propriete.org/english/2004/2004download_pdf/Benjamin2004.pdf

24. http://nces.ed.gov/fastfacts/display.asp?id=66